T0358547

Routledge Revivals

Industrial Employment and Unemployment in West Yorkshire

First Published in 1936, *Industrial Employment and Unemployment in West Yorkshire* presents the trends of employment and unemployment on the basis of official statistics. West Yorkshire is in many respects a representative British industrial region. Though not enjoying as great prosperity as London and the South Midlands, it has escaped the severe depression experienced in Lancashire, South Wales, Scotland, and the North of England. The position in the predepression years, the magnitude of the depression and the course of the recovery are brought under review. These changes inevitably affect the industrial structure of an area. An estimate is made of the surplus of labour in the area and of the possibility of reabsorbing this surplus into industry. This book is an essential archival resource for scholars and researchers of British economy, labour economics, labour history and economics in general.

Industrial Employment and Unemployment in West Yorkshire

A Statistical Review of Recent Trends

J. Henry Richardson

Routledge
Taylor & Francis Group

First published in 1936
by George Allen & Unwin Ltd.

This edition first published in 2022 by Routledge
2 Park Square, Milton Park, Abingdon, Oxon, OX14 4RN
and by Routledge
605 Third Avenue, New York, NY 10017

Routledge is an imprint of the Taylor & Francis Group, an informa business

© 1936 J. Henry Richardson

All rights reserved. No part of this book may be reprinted or reproduced or utilised in any form or by any electronic, mechanical, or other means, now known or hereafter invented, including photocopying and recording, or in any information storage or retrieval system, without permission in writing from the publishers.

Publisher's Note
The publisher has gone to great lengths to ensure the quality of this reprint but points out that some imperfections in the original copies may be apparent.

Disclaimer
The publisher has made every effort to trace copyright holders and welcomes correspondence from those they have been unable to contact.

A Library of Congress record exists under LCCN:

ISBN: 978-1-032-18301-5 (hbk)
ISBN: 978-1-003-25396-9 (ebk)
ISBN: 978-1-032-18302-2 (pbk)

Book DOI 10.4324/9781003253969

INDUSTRIAL EMPLOYMENT
AND UNEMPLOYMENT
IN WEST YORKSHIRE

A STATISTICAL REVIEW
OF RECENT TRENDS

by

J. Henry Richardson, M.A., PH.D.

Montague Burton Professor of Industrial
Relations in the University of Leeds

LONDON

GEORGE ALLEN & UNWIN LTD

MUSEUM STREET

FIRST PUBLISHED IN 1936

All rights reserved

PRINTED IN GREAT BRITAIN BY
UNWIN BROTHERS LTD., WOKING

PREFACE

WEST YORKSHIRE is an area with distinctive economic features and industrial unity. As in other parts of the country, changes in standards of living and in the ways in which people spend their incomes, together with the changes in methods of production, the wide fluctuations of trade and the restrictions in foreign markets during recent years, are altering the industrial structure of West Yorkshire, and it is useful to examine these trends systematically. The present study reviews the problem of employment and unemployment in West Yorkshire industries on the basis of official statistics. It also serves as an introduction—the only one available—to the industrial structure of West Yorkshire.

The statistics used have been mainly supplied by the Ministry of Labour, and special thanks are due to Mr. E. C. Ramsbottom, O.B.E., Director of Statistics, and to his colleagues both at headquarters and at the North-Eastern Divisional Office in Leeds for making available a large amount of information. Thanks are also due to Mr. R. K. Bacon, Mr. W. Prest, Mr. J. N. Reedman, and Mr. N. Collindridge for undertaking investigations, the results of which have been utilized in several sections

of the review, and to Mr. K. G. T. Clark for writing
a section on the geographical background and for
preparing a map of the area.

J. HENRY RICHARDSON

THE UNIVERSITY, LEEDS
October 1936

CONTENTS

INDUSTRIAL EMPLOYMENT AND UNEMPLOYMENT IN WEST YORKSHIRE

I

INTRODUCTION

THERE is a great economic and social value in the systematic study of the industrial structure and development of an area. In the ordinary course of their daily activities the people living in a locality know that its prosperity is based upon certain industries. They have a general impression that trade is improving or declining, and may recognize that some industries are becoming more prosperous, while others are leaving the locality owing to the competition of other districts or of other countries, or are dwindling as a result of diminution of demand. These impressions are, however, often vague and inexact. Even business men, while fully aware of the factors directly affecting their own industry and undertakings, are not always adequately informed about the trends of other industries in the district which may indirectly contribute to the expansion or contraction of their trade.

During recent years industrial and social surveys have been undertaken in various parts of Great

Britain with the object of giving a systematic picture of existing conditions, examining the trends of development, and estimating the needs and future prospects of a defined industrial region. Some of these have been voluntary, for example the very detailed *Survey of London Life and Labour* compiled under the direction of Sir Hubert Llewelyn Smith. Others owe their origin to the desire of the Government for information about industrial conditions and prospects in districts suffering from exceptionally severe unemployment, and for this purpose collaboration was arranged between Government Departments and various universities, which resulted in the publication of surveys of South Wales, Lancashire, Tyneside, and Clydeside.

A number of important industrial areas of the country have not hitherto been brought under review. Yet information about these areas is of great interest both to those living there, and also to complete the review of conditions throughout the country. The statistics published by Government Departments for Great Britain often merge local conditions into a composite picture. In this way many realities are overlooked and it is desirable that nation-wide information should be completed by more detailed regional and local information.

Hitherto no systematic survey of industrial conditions has been made in West Yorkshire. This area has many special characteristics, which make it a particularly interesting field for investigation. It has not suffered from the exceptionally severe unemployment experienced in the more depressed parts of the country. On the other hand, it has not enjoyed the remarkable prosperity during post-war years of the southern and midland areas. Standing in an intermediate position between considerable prosperity and severe depression, it may be regarded as in some respects a typical or representative British industrial region. While containing certain specially important highly localized industries, such as the woollen and worsted trades, an important feature is the variety of its industries. It is largely because of this variety that West Yorkshire has been spared the very severe depression experienced by certain districts which are dependent upon a more specialized industrial structure.

The present review makes no pretence to be an industrial survey or even a detailed survey of employment and unemployment in the chief industries of West Yorkshire. Such investigations could only be undertaken by a team of qualified research workers. In 1934 a research group, consisting of members of the staff of the Economics Department of the University of Leeds in association with members of other departments of the University and with several investigators not on the University staff, decided to undertake a comprehensive survey of employment and unemployment in West Yorkshire. Subsequently, however, the group reached the conclusion that, on a voluntary basis without substantial financial resources, such a survey could not be successfully completed.

In the course of preliminary investigations for the intended survey a considerable amount of information was collected, particularly some hitherto unpublished statistics of employment and unemployment supplied by the Ministry of Labour. These statistics, which are of considerable interest and merit publication, form the basis of the present review. They enable the trends of employment and unemployment to be traced for most of the postwar period, including the great depression; they indicate the expanding and declining industries, and enable an estimate to be made of the future prospects of employment in the area. The present time, when substantial progress has been made towards recovery, is appropriate for a review of the situation resulting from the wide industrial fluctuations of recent years.

During the worst period of the depression the number of adult insured workpeople unemployed in the twelve chief towns of West Yorkshire reached a total of over 113,000. Subsequently the recovery resulted in a reduction of the number to 55,000 in May 1936. Such great disturbances cannot leave industry unchanged, and it is of interest to examine the present position of the industries of West Yorkshire, from the point of view of the employment they give, compared with that in pre-depression years.

II

THE AREA UNDER REVIEW

(a) BOUNDARIES, POPULATION, AND CHIEF INDUSTRIES

WEST YORKSHIRE—the area selected for study—is a compact industrial agglomeration in the middle of the West Riding. Its chief centres are Leeds and Bradford. Keighley, Halifax, and Huddersfield form its western boundary; the line then runs east to Wakefield and Pontefract, and thence north-west to Castleford and Leeds and on through Shipley to Keighley. In addition to the towns already mentioned, the area includes Dewsbury, Spenborough, Morley, Batley, Brighouse, Rothwell, Normanton, Bingley, Elland, Ossett, Pudsey, Mirfield, Horsforth, and a number of smaller centres. It has features which give it an industrial character of its own, and it forms a distinct economic unit separated in many ways from the neighbouring industrial area in the south of the West Riding which includes Sheffield, Barnsley, Doncaster, and Rotherham.

Geographically, industrial West Yorkshire consists mainly of the valleys of the middle Aire to the north and the Calder towards the south, together with the Colne valley and the area lying between these river lines. It is roughly triangular in shape,

the longest side being from Pontefract to Keighley—
a distance of about 30 miles. The area comprises a
total of about 295 square miles. The boundaries,
general geographical features, and the distribution
of the towns in the area are indicated in the map
opposite.

The boundaries of the area have necessarily been
fixed arbitrarily, and certain towns have been
excluded which are linked industrially more or less
closely with the area. Among these towns are Todmorden, Sowerby Bridge, Skipton, Guiseley, Otley,
Harrogate, and Ilkley. Some of these towns, e.g.
Todmorden, are excluded because, although in the
West Riding, their industries are closely associated
with those of Lancashire. Other towns, e.g. Harrogate and Ilkley, are excluded because, while intimately related to the West Yorkshire industrial towns, they are themselves residential and not
industrial. Emphasis may again be laid upon
the compact unity of the industrial area under
review.

The total population of the area at the time of
the 1931 Census was about one and a half million
persons, or rather more than one-thirtieth of the
population of Great Britain. The number of persons
to the square mile is about 5,100 in West Yorkshire,
compared with about 505 in Great Britain. The
statistics of employment and unemployment upon
which this study is based cover the twelve largest

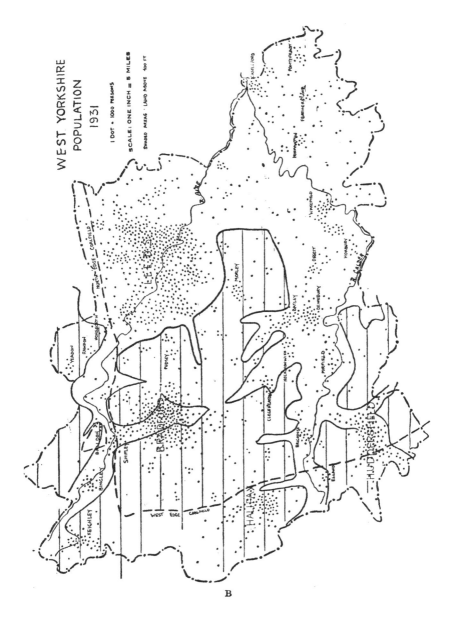

WEST YORKSHIRE
POPULATION
1931

1 DOT = 1000 PERSONS

SCALE: ONE INCH = 5 MILES

SHADED AREAS - LAND ABOVE 400 FT

B

towns of the area.[1] These towns, with a population in 1931 of 1,306,320 persons, cover about 85 per cent of the total number of persons living in the area. They, therefore, provide an adequate basis for a study of employment and unemployment in the whole of West Yorkshire.

Census figures of the populations of these towns in 1911, 1921, and 1931 are given in the table opposite. They show an increase of over 34,000 or 2·7 per cent in the population of the twelve towns together during the twenty years from 1911 to 1931, most of this increase taking place during the second half of the period. Wakefield shows the most rapid rate of increase, followed by Shipley, Leeds, and Huddersfield. Keighley, Castleford, and Batley show the most marked fall in population of 5 to 7 per cent. In both Batley and Castleford the decline took place almost entirely after 1921.

West Yorkshire has a wide variety of industries, and, in Section v dealing with expanding and contracting industries, statistics are given for nearly fifty industries of considerable importance. More detailed information is given in Section vi for nine of the chief industries. These are the following, the figures being the estimated numbers of insured

[1] These twelve towns are Leeds, Bradford, Huddersfield, Halifax, Wakefield, Castleford, Dewsbury, Keighley, Spenborough, Shipley, Morley, and Batley. The statistical information is largely limited to these towns in order to avoid a considerable addition to the work of the Ministry of Labour in extracting figures for the smaller towns from detailed returns.

POPULATION OF TWELVE WEST YORKSHIRE TOWNS ACCORDING TO THE CENSUS STATISTICS, 1911, 1921 AND 1931

	1911	1921	1931 Number	1931 Percentage increase (+) or decrease (−) since 1911
Batley	36,389	36,137	34,573	− 5·0
Bradford	293,321	291,004	298,041	+ 1·6
Castleford	23,090	24,185	21,784	− 5·7
Dewsbury	53,351	54,160	54,302	+ 1·8
Halifax	101,594	99,183	98,115	− 3·4
Huddersfield	107,821	110,102	113,475	+ 5·2
Keighley	43,487	41,921	40,441	− 7·0
Leeds	458,823	463,122	482,809	+ 5·2
Morley	24,282	23,934	23,396	− 3·6
Shipley	27,706	28,277	30,242	+ 9·2
Spenborough	31,320	31,117	30,963	− 1·2
Wakefield	51,666	53,052	59,122	+ 14·4
Totals	1,252,850	1,256,194	1,287,263	+ 2·7

persons aged 16 to 64 in each industry in the twelve chief towns of West Yorkshire at July 1935:

Wool and worsted	.. ..	140,000
Distributive trades	.. ..	65,700
Tailoring	.. ..	47,750
General engineering	.. ..	36,850
Coal mining	.. ..	34,350*
Building	.. ..	27,000
Road transport†	..	13,350
Printing and bookbinding	..	11,720
Textile dyeing, etc.	.. ..	11,500

* This figure includes Pontefract in addition to the numbers for the twelve chief towns.

† Tramway, omnibus, and other road transport.

These nine industries cover about 70 per cent of the total number of insured persons in all the industries in the twelve chief towns. The woollen and worsted industry predominates; its predominance is still more marked if the allied industries of textile dyeing and finishing, and tailoring are included with it.

(*b*) GEOGRAPHICAL BACKGROUND

By K. G. T. CLARK, Geography Department, Leeds University.

The area embraced by this review is somewhat more extensive than the urban agglomeration to which the title of "West Yorkshire" is by custom attached, since it includes industrial areas which represent satellites of the main concentrations of population and also tracts marginal to the industrial nucleus which help to satisfy the latter's demand for essential raw materials and foodstuffs. The greater part of the region, however, has a recognizable individuality from the viewpoint of economic development, because of its centuries-old association with specialization in producing woollen goods. To-day this specialization is more apparent in the cultural landscape than in the picture which may be drawn from data given in the occupational census. The complexity of social and economic life in areas associated with factory industry gives rise to varied organizations which cater for the industrial population or are essential to the progress of any economic specialization. These include transport facilities and commercial and financial businesses, which tend to absorb an increasing proportion of the working population. Nevertheless, in the larger urban units within the West Yorkshire region, one-tenth to one-sixth of the populations concerned are to-day directly employed in producing textile fabrics or in converting such fabrics into clothing and other finished goods.

As already indicated, the largest urban groupings within this area are Leeds, Bradford, Huddersfield, and Halifax. It will be seen from the map on page 17 that none of these occupies a nodal position for the industrial region as a whole. However, although there is no centre which, geometrically speaking, is a focus, Leeds is predominant in certain branches of distribution in the area as a whole, while Bradford occupies an outstanding position in the wool trade. In this Yorkshire region many of the larger towns are peripheral to the urbanized area as a whole. This feature of arrangement of settlement must be related in part to the general character of the geographical ground-plan of the region. Essential elements in this are two eastward-opening valleys occupied by the Aire and Calder rivers. These valleys, together with their well-developed tributary systems, are cut out of an old plateau surface which loses height towards the Vale of York. The "built-up" areas which are a product of the factory age are sedimented for the most part within the valleys, spread out "ribbon-like" along their often confined floors. In view of the fact that the relatively high land which forms the watershed between the Aire and Calder systems extends centrally west-east through the urban area there tends to be a zone of relatively low density of population across the centre of the region.

This "altitude-control" upon settlement distribution is more apparent than real. In certain parts of the region, particularly towards the west, the distribution of settlements, varying in character from hamlets to significant towns, shows features which suggest defiance of disadvantages generally associated with increasing altitude. The settlements are often perched on ledges well above the valley floors or upon the high surface of the gently dipping grit-stones which mantle the old plateau surface, and hence near where agriculturally productive land gives place to cotton-grass or heather moor. In such parts the "built-up" area represents at least two major strata of settlement, differentiated in place and time. The modern growth is for the most part in the valleys. An older phase has escaped obliteration largely because of a change in site values which materialized with the progress of the industrial revolution. The "museum" of structures related to the domestic stage of industry exists on the hills.[1] The few elements of this period which occupied strategic points in the valley bottoms have been submerged under the mushroom growth of the modern built-up areas. To-day the relics of the past are in greater danger of at least partial destruction by the tendency for areas of residence to become spacially divorced from areas of work by the claiming of relatively high ground for house-building.

The old hillside nuclei are a reminder that, from at least the time of Mercian colonization of West Yorkshire south of the Wharfe down to the time of the break up of the domestic system in the woollen industry, one may trace continuity of settlement of many hillside sites. Ill drained land and the prevailing vegetation of oak, sycamore, and wych-elm forest or woodland repelled early settlement from the floors of the valleys. Examination of maps representing conditions even at the middle of the

[1] See W. B. Crump and G. Ghorbal, *History of the Huddersfield Woollen Industry*.

eighteenth century show how, in general, settlements
and roads avoided the main valley bottoms. The
physical character of the landscape and its climatic
conditions make the grit country and the higher
western part of the coal measures inherently poor
farming land except when kept under grass. Thus
within the western part of this West Yorkshire
region the establishment of prosperous self-sufficing
agricultural communities was in medieval times
virtually impossible. Conditions mitigated against
feudal agrarian organization finding full expression
here and disintegration, involving enclosures, was
in the main early. Disintegration brought into being
a virile yeoman class who established themselves
along the higher valley slopes, often taking up battle
with the apparently unresponsive moorland.

It was natural in view of environmental circumstances that this yeoman class should look for some
form of activity to supplement their small return
from the soil. Various factors stimulated attention
towards specialization upon the production of
woollen cloths. At various levels on the hillsides,
thanks to the alternation of sandstones and shales,
spring lines occur, giving soft water useful for
washing and dyeing wool. The Cistercian monasteries created increased interest in wool production
and cloth-making. The gradual decay of the older
centres of specialization such as York and Beverley
made room for expansion farther to the west. The
dissolution of the monasteries gave the opportunity

for many of the more prosperous yeomen-clothiers to acquire land and provide more fulling mills— the earliest valley floor element in the industry. The domestic industry passed from strength to strength, and it leaves evidence of its prosperity at a late stage in the many substantial clothiers' homes which still exist and, less pretentious in character, in the weaving cottages and hamlets with their mullioned windows behind which the hand-looms were worked. Cloth halls, pack-horse trails, and eighteenth-century stoops provide reminders of the organization of marketing related to the internal and external trade of the region.

It has been suggested above that inherently poor environmental circumstances stimulated interest in what became the dominant economic specialization of the district. The maturation of the woollen industry from the domestic stage to that of factory organization was, however, facilitated by local positive advantages. Resources of the district previously but scantily exploited became of primary significance. Especially important was the dissected nature of the uplands lying to the west of the woollen region and the presence of coal and ironstone in immediate proximity to the area traditionally associated with the woollen industry.

Corridors through the Pennines gave easy contact with the South Lancashire plain. Along these filtered technological ideas applicable to the woollen industry, and into them the cotton manufacturing industry spread, displacing the woollen industry eastwards. The corridors also provided routes suitable for roads, canals, and railways as the need arose for linking West Yorkshire with ocean termini on the opposite side of the Pennines.

With the coming of the machine age previously almost unoccupied sites assumed real value. The old valley foci associated with the fulling mills and bridges became the nuclei around which the scribbling mills and the work of spinning tended to congregate. New techniques were worked out along the valley bottoms. Bi-focal settlements grew up in many parts. Thus the old hillside groupings such as Birstall, Gomersall, Haworth, Baildon, and Marsden grew counterparts in the neighbouring vales. A divorce took place between spinning and weaving, the latter tending to cling to the hills long after the centre of gravity of the former had moved to riverside or canal-side locations.

There was a considerable period between the establishment of a pseudo-factory organization and the adoption of steam power. When the latter took a grip of the industry the days of the upland weaving settlements seemed numbered. Threat of decay varied, however, on a regional basis. In the grit country there are no coal seams of economic worth, and high-level weaving centres found difficulty in obtaining the new essential fuel at reasonable cost. Recognition of their difficulty and the spirit aroused in some areas by struggle for survival found expression in attempts to ensure and to improve the local water power resources by reservoir construction. Eastwards, however, in the coal measures region, workable coal seams were often found at considerable altitudes, thus facilitating the maintenance of the localization of weaving units and in some cases encouraging new ventures at high levels. On the whole, however, as the significance of valley transport facilities became apparent, the various branches of the woollen industry tended to develop in ribbon fashion along canal, river, road, and rail within the main valleys and their better defined tributaries.

From very early times there must have been a certain trade between the poor grit-stone country and the richer coal measures areas. To the farmer the latter were always intrinsically more productive. Thus centres of exchange which grew into market towns tended to develop near the junction of these contrasted regions where the grit-stone valleys opened out into the less hilly coal measures districts. The presence of coal and ironstone outcropping in close proximity to old-established market towns roughly along the line of the junction was a factor which tended to maintain the significance of old centres when machines and steam-power were accepted. Individual interest and initiative ensured that the woollen industry did not leave its traditional home in the grit country, but it was natural that in the modern age expansion should take place within the coal-bearing area. One must visualize, therefore, the centre of gravity of the woollen industry as a whole moving eastwards, but much less significantly than the centre of gravity of the coal-mining industry. Thus as time has gone on the area of wool-textile industry has tended to become distinct from that supplying the bulk of its chief source of power.

The growth of modern factory organization has synchronized with the full development of specialization in various types of woollen fabrics, each having its special features of localization which are often the result of historical accident or individual initiative rather than of the relative natural advantages of each locality.

In this recent period great diversity of industry has grown up within the West Yorkshire region. Premium has been placed on an ever-widening range of locally obtainable raw materials. The coal industry has already been mentioned. Its eastward migration has involved tapping the seams in country where the coal measures dip beneath younger strata, superficially giving a sporadic industrial character to a landscape which till recently was essentially rural. The coal measures have also yielded important raw materials in the form of ganister and fireclays, whilst layers of ironstone provided a basis for initiating iron-working, which, aided by imported raw materials and a local market, gave rise to specialized engineering enterprise.

The area abounds in building stones, which until

very recent times enabled many of the built-up areas to convey the impression of being one with the land on which they lay. Finally West Yorkshire is encircled, notably to north and west, by country admirably suited, owing particularly to the veneer of watertight glacial material in its valleys and its considerable rainfall, to the construction of reservoirs to provide the water supply essential for industry and domestic consumption.

Farming throughout the centuries has maintained, in a large part of this region, only a precarious existence. Except in the eastern tracts, natural circumstances favour a pastoral bias. Speaking generally, it may be said that conditions in the grit-stone country preclude arable farming except in sheltered pockets or at times of unusual demand and high prices. It has been pointed out that small-holdings early became characteristic in the grit country with the decay of manorial organization. They became a feature in the coal measures country with the development of the industrial revolution. Industrialization has reacted powerfully upon local farming. It gave for a time great advantages, even in the face of rising land values, because of the possibility of supplying a rapidly growing local demand for farm products. But the advantages of nearness to markets have been much reduced and must be weighed against serious difficulties, which to a large extent are a by-product of industrialization. The rapidity with which demand for various products has

changed as consumers have become more dis-
criminating calls for a measure of adaptability by the
farmer which, particularly in animal husbandry, is
virtually impossible to achieve.

Industrialization has intensified the tendency for
the local soils to suffer from acidity. This fact and
the atmospheric conditions often prevailing have
injurious effects upon certain crops and the breeding
of cattle. With the growth of rapid and compara-
tively cheap transport facilities the farmers of the
industrialized districts naturally experience intensified competition from adjacent rural areas as
well as from abroad. Only towards the eastern side
of West Yorkshire could the reorganization of farming associated with the agrarian revolution be fully
effected. The post-war period here has seen cus-
tomary systems abolished through the necessity of
producing for the market of the moment with consequent neglect of maintenance of the land in its best
condition. Here the development of coal-mining has
brought in its train problems related to subsidence,
and not a few farmers find compensation from
colliery companies a valuable item on their balance
sheet.

During the decade preceding the last census (1931)
the population of West Yorkshire increased by
approximately 3·5 per cent as compared with an
increase of 5·4 per cent for England and Wales as
a whole. The rate of growth of population in this
area is notably lower than in the decennial periods

1891–1901 (8·2 per cent) and 1901–1911 (4·2 per cent). The period 1911–1921 is not comparable because of the effects of the Great War. The region is an urbanized area in which the birth-rate has declined during the last half-century at a more rapid rate than in the majority of regions of similar character in other parts of the country. It has also shared with other large urban agglomerations over the last thirty years the characteristic of being an area in which the growth of population has been less than the natural increase, an indication of migration, involving the relief of congested industrial nuclei by decentralization of industry giving rise to marginal areas of residence and work. This process of population redistribution is, however, not purely one of marginal shifts; it involves long-distance movements, the net results of which are that the old industrial areas of the north and north-west Midlands are losing by migration to Greater London and the Home Counties. This migratory movement has been much smaller from West Yorkshire than from the specially depressed areas of the country.

GENERAL TREND OF EMPLOYMENT
AND UNEMPLOYMENT

WEST YORKSHIRE provides employment for about one-twentieth of the insured population of the country. The total number of insured workpeople in West Yorkshire is about 680,000, compared with just over 13,000,000 in Great Britain and Northern Ireland, and the number in the twelve chief towns of West Yorkshire is nearly 550,000.[1]

The table opposite shows for recent years the estimated total number of insured adult persons between the ages of 18 and 64 in the twelve chief industrial towns, and the number of these persons in employment. The statistics show an increase of over 7 per cent in the number of insured adult workpeople during the period from 1924 to 1936. In the summer of 1936 the number of these workpeople in employment was slightly greater than in any other year. However, this number formed a smaller

[1] In order to obtain the total number of workpeople in the area there should be added persons not covered by the unemployment insurance statistics, chiefly agricultural workers, domestic servants, various categories of railway workers in permanent employment, and non-manual workers in receipt of remuneration at a rate of over £250 a year. For agricultural workers a scheme of unemployment insurance is being introduced, but detailed statistics of employment and unemployment are not yet available for these workers.

percentage of the numbers insured than in the years before the depression. In view of improvements in the efficiency of industry during recent years the volume or production in West Yorkshire must now be greater

NUMBER AND EMPLOYMENT OF INSURED ADULT
WORKPEOPLE IN TWELVE WEST YORKSHIRE
TOWNS, 1924 TO 1936*

Year	Number of Insured Adults†	EMPLOYMENT OF INSURED ADULTS‡ Number	Percentage of Number Insured
1924	475,270	447,410	94·2
1928	484,420	440,620	91·0
1929	484,160	431,790	89·2
1930	493,590	406,700	82·4
1931	504,660	396,690	78·6
1932	500,160	386,400	77·3
1933	502,870	406,550	80·9
1934	504,740	426,500	84·5
1935	507,680	434,340	85·5
1936	510,000§	454,830§	89·2

* The comparability of the statistics for different years is somewhat affected by administrative changes, but the figures are adequate for the purpose of indicating general trends.
† Statistics for July of each year.
‡ Statistics for May of each year. The figures are obtained by deducting the numbers unemployed in May from the numbers insured (July estimates).   § Provisional estimates.

than ever before. During the height of the depression, in 1931 and 1932, less than 80 per cent of insured adult workpeople were in employment. In the worst year of the depression between 50,000 and 60,000 fewer adult workpeople were engaged in production than in the pre-depression years 1924 and 1928,

In reviewing the statistics of unemployment, it is

useful to distinguish as far as possible between:
(1) unemployment due to ordinary or regular
causes operative each year, including seasonal variations, normal turnover of workpeople moving to
other jobs, firms in process of contraction or going
out of business, and workpeople bordering on the
unemployable; (2) unemployment due to trade
cycle depressions; (3) unemployment due to special
causes, e.g. raising of trade barriers abroad, changes
in fashion, long period decline in demand. The
numbers in the first of these categories can be
estimated fairly easily, but the second and third
categories are more difficult to separate. At the high
points of the trade cycle the number of workpeople
unemployed from cyclical causes becomes negligible.
It is by studying the numbers in the third category
that conclusions may be drawn as to whether a
district is suffering from a long-range surplus of
labour.

It has been estimated that since the war the
amount of unemployment in Great Britain in the
first category, which may be termed normal or
"minimum" unemployment, is not less than 5½ per
cent of the total number of workpeople.[1] In West
Yorkshire, with its high proportion of seasonal

[1] Five and a half per cent is probably an underestimate, as
allowance must be made for the fact that the peaks of seasonal
unemployment occur at different parts of the year for different
industries, e.g. coal in summer and building in winter, and each
industry must have its own reserve of labour to meet the needs
of periods of high seasonal demand.

trades, the percentage of normal or "minimum" unemployment is about 6 or 6½, representing at the present time about 40,000 to 44,000 persons.[1] In other words, unemployment is not likely to fall below this figure, even in favourable periods of the trade cycle. It would only be less if special factors were operating to create an abnormal demand for labour, for example, the application of a rearmament programme considerably greater than at present. In the summer of 1936 the number unemployed from cyclical causes was small, probably not more than a few thousands.

The general position as shown by statistics for the twelve chief towns may be examined in some detail. For these towns, data are given in the table below of the total numbers of insured adults between the ages of 18 and 64 who were recorded as unemployed at various dates during the period from 1924 to 1936. The percentages which these numbers represent of the total number of insured adults are also given, and percentages for the whole country are added for purposes of comparison.

The smallest number of unemployed persons during the period covered by the table was in May, 1924.[2] A figure of 27,860 was recorded in that

[1] This is calculated from a total number of insured workpeople of 680,000.

[2] May and November for which figures are given in the table are months of good seasonal employment, when the numbers unemployed compare favourably with those in most other months in each half of the year.

NUMBERS AND PERCENTAGES OF INSURED PER-
SONS, AGED 18 TO 64 YEARS, RECORDED AS UN-
EMPLOYED IN THE TWELVE LARGEST TOWNS
OF WEST YORKSHIRE, AND PERCENTAGES FOR
THE WHOLE COUNTRY, 1924 TO 1936*

	TWELVE WEST YORKSHIRE TOWNS		WHOLE COUNTRY†
Date	*Number Unemployed*	*Percentage*	*Percentage*
1924			
May	27,860	5·8	9·4
November	43,560	9·1	10·9
1928			
May	43,803	9·0	9·8
November	66,050	13·6	12·1
1929			
May	52,371	10·8	9·7
November	66,465	13·7	10·9
1930			
May	86,875	17·6	15·0
November	108,872	22·1	19·1
1931			
May	107,974	21·4	20·2
November	105,697	20·9	21·4
1932			
May	113,765	22·7	22·0
November	113,653	22·7	22·2
1933			
May	96,325	19·1	19·4
November	79,454	15·8	17·9
1934			
May	78,238	15·5	16·2
November	77,686	15·4	16·4
1935			
May	73,340	14·5	15·5
November	62,812	12·4	14·6
1936			
May	55,170	10·8‡	13·0

* As the percentages for West Yorkshire are calculated by
using the estimated number of insured persons in July of each
year, and as these numbers have tended to increase from year
to year, the percentages given for May are probably slightly
too low, and those for November somewhat too high, but
they are adequate to indicate the general trend.

† Great Britain and Northern Ireland. These figures include juveniles aged 16 to 18 years.   ‡ Provisional.

month, the percentage being only 5·8. This figure almost entirely represented normal or minimum unemployment, the numbers unemployed from cyclical and special causes being small.[1] In May 1928, which was near the peak of the trade cycle, the number recorded as unemployed was 43,803. Of these around 30,000 represented normal unemployment, and among the remainder it may be estimated that over 10,000 were unemployed owing to special causes, including decline in demand for coal, and difficulties in foreign trade which particularly affected the woollen industry.

The worst year of the depression was 1932, when more than 113,000 adult insured persons were unemployed in May, and also in November in the twelve towns. About 32,000 of these were unemployed from "normal" causes. Of the remainder, about one-half, or some 40,000 adult workpeople, were out of work as a result of trade cycle factors, while the unemployment of a similar number was due to special factors. The next three years showed steady recovery, and this was accelerated during the autumn of 1935 and in 1936 largely owing to maintenance of building activity at a high level, but also to growth of confidence resulting from increase in general purchasing power, and to the

[1] In 1924 an appreciable number of persons who in recent years would have been reckoned as unemployed were excluded as a result of the administrative principles then applied.

indirect as well as direct effects of the rearmament programme.

By May 1936 unemployment among adults in the twelve towns under consideration had fallen to 55,170, representing an unemployment percentage of under 11. This was about 11,000, or 1·8 per cent, more than in the corresponding month of the pre-depression year, 1928. Approximately 33,000 were unemployed from "normal" causes. Only a small number—probably not more than five thousand—were suffering from cyclical unemployment, and this is the number likely to be reabsorbed into industry as a result of further progress in cyclical recovery. The remainder—about 17,000 or 3·3 per cent—were unemployed from special causes, including persistent long-range depression in coal-mining, and decline of certain industries in the area (e.g. locomotive engineering) owing to migration of manufacture to other parts of the country, or long-range obstacles to export trade.

Allowing for unemployment in the smaller towns, the total number of workers in West Yorkshire who may be considered surplus to the needs of existing industries and services in a period of good cyclical trade is probably about 18,000 to 20,000. This number is very much smaller than the figures estimated for the specially depressed areas of the country. It consists mainly of men, as long-range unemployment is very small among women and juveniles. The existence of this surplus is in no way incompatible with shortage of certain skilled categories of workers in various industries.

The two main alternatives for dealing with this surplus are transfer to other districts, or absorption into expanding industries in West Yorkshire itself. Movement of workers away from West Yorkshire and of workers into West Yorkshire from other districts is a continuous process, and the two movements seem to be fairly evenly balanced. Given maintenance of reasonably good trade conditions, West Yorkshire should experience little difficulty by business developments during the next ten or twelve years in absorbing into industry most of the workpeople who are, under present conditions, surplus to her needs.[1]

In concluding this section, trends of unemployment in West Yorkshire during the last twelve years may be compared with changes in the country as a whole. For this purpose the two series of percentages given in the preceding table may be used. They show that before the depression the position in West Yorkshire was more favourable than that in the whole country. West Yorkshire was affected earlier, and the depression was more severe than in the country generally. Once recovery began, however, it proceeded more rapidly in West Yorkshire than in the country as a whole, and since 1933 West Yorkshire has had a smaller burden of unemployment

[1] Account should be taken of the effect of declining birthrate upon the number of the working population.

than the average of all districts. This is, no doubt, due largely to the fact that West Yorkshire is less dependent than many parts of the country upon the export trade, and that Britain's recovery has been much greater in home markets than in those abroad. It may also be noted that, according to the experience of the last twelve years, West Yorkshire enjoys a better record in good times than the country as a whole, but suffers more severely in years of depression. In other words, fluctuations are wider than in Britain generally. This is due in part to the fact that West Yorkshire, though not so highly specialized as some districts, is dependent for prosperity upon a smaller number of industries than the whole country, and benefits less from the compensations resulting from a more diversified industrial structure.

IV

TRENDS IN CHIEF TOWNS[1]

THE number of insured workpeople shows a general upward trend during the last ten or twelve years in West Yorkshire as a whole, an increase of 3·8 per cent in the twelve chief towns, corresponding closely with the growth of population during the same period. The experience of the different towns, however, deviates considerably from this general trend. The outstanding change is marked increase in the number of insured workpeople in Leeds, the total in 1935 being nearly 30,000 more than in 1924. Had it not been for this increase, West Yorkshire as a whole would have recorded a decline. Wakefield, Halifax, Dewsbury, and Huddersfield show small increases, while Bradford remains almost stationary. All the other towns show appreciable declines, the change being greatest in Shipley, Morley, Castleford, and Batley. The greatest reduction in numbers though not in percentage was in the coal-mining centre of Castleford, which has suffered from a decade of depression, this being reflected in a fall of about 3,500 in the number of insured workpeople. It is significant that the large centres have generally maintained their position better than the smaller towns under review.

[1] In drawing conclusions from the statistics of insured persons in different towns, account should be taken of the note on their significance given in Appendix I.

These conclusions are based upon the statistics tabulated below, which show the estimated numbers of insured persons between the ages of 16 and 64 in each of the twelve chief centres of the area at July 1924 and July 1935. The figures include unemployed workpeople. If these were deducted from the numbers insured, in order to compare the numbers of insured workpeople in employment, the percentage increases would be somewhat smaller and the percentage decreases somewhat greater than those shown in the table, as there was more unemployment in 1935 than in 1924.

ESTIMATED NUMBERS OF INSURED PERSONS AGED 16 TO 64 IN THE CHIEF TOWNS OF WEST YORKSHIRE, AT JULY 1924 AND JULY 1935

Town	NUMBER OF INSURED PERSONS		*Percentage increase (+) or decrease (−)*
	July 1924	*July 1935*	
Leeds	155,240	184,460	+ 18·8
Wakefield	29,220	30,210	+ 3·4
Halifax	38,760	39,960	+ 3·1
Dewsbury	20,050	20,260	+ 1·0
Huddersfield	51,460	51,900	+ 0·9
Bradford	117,350	116,660	− 0·6
Spenborough	17,180	16,800	− 2·3
Keighley	18,970	17,630	− 7·1
Shipley	14,860	13,330	− 10·3
Morley	15,530	13,360	− 14·0
Castleford	25,150	21,620	− 14·0
Batley	15,330	12,810	− 16·4
Total, twelve centres	519,100	539,000	+ 3·8

V

EXPANDED AND CONTRACTED
INDUSTRIES

THERE are various ways of determining whether an industry is expanding, remaining stationary, or contracting. In the present review the test applied is the number of insured workpeople in employment. It should be noted, however, that an industry may be expanding its production while continuing to employ the same number or even a smaller number of workpeople, owing to the introduction of labour-saving methods and machinery. There is considerable evidence that during the depression the productivity per head of workpeople has increased and that, especially in coal-mining and in certain branches of engineering, labour-saving methods have been applied. This tendency indicates the need, if the employment capacity of West Yorkshire is to be maintained, for the continuous opening up of new fields of employment, by expansion of existing industries and establishment of new ones to find jobs which will compensate for those lost in industries maintaining or increasing their production with a smaller labour force or suffering from declining demand.

Changes in the relative numbers of workpeople in different industries are due mainly to decline in

EXPANDED INDUSTRIES

Industry	Numbers in Employment			Percentages in 1934 and 1935 compared with 1923 (= 100)	
	1923	1934	1935	1934	1935
Electrical engineering	957	2,420	2,704	252·9	282·6
Electric wiring and contracting	441	1,095	1,086	248·3	246·3
Laundries, dry cleaning, etc.	2,392	4,447	5,413	185·9	226·3
Tramway and omnibus service	3,503	6,614	7,107	188·8	202·9
Entertainments and sports	2,190	2,882	4,418	131·6	201·7
Brick, tile, etc., making	1,668	3,167	3,304	189·9	198·1
Road transport*	2,720	4,905	5,246	180·3	192·9
Artificial silk	2,720	4,539	4,446	166·9	163·5
Distributive trades	39,309	61,135	60,532	155·5	154·0
Professional services	3,212	5,038	4,877	156·8	151·8
Motor vehicles, cycles, and aircraft	2,908	4,668	4,348	160·5	149·5
Bread, cakes, etc.	3,082	3,827	4,400	124·2	142·8
Tailoring	32,175	43,504	45,591	135·2	141·7
Building	17,779	22,609	23,477	127·2	132·0
Hotels, public houses, restaurants, boarding houses, etc.	4,177	5,412	5,397	129·6	129·2

Printing, publishing, etc.	..	..	8,392	10,552	10,556	125·7	125·7
Glass trades ..	..	..	1,423	1,775	1,738	124·7	122·1
Brass and allied metal wares	..	..	1,587	1,807	1,885	113·7	118·8
Clothing trades†	..	..	3,426	4,155	4,048	121·3	118·2
Furniture making	..	..	4,021	4,837	4,739	123·3	117·9
Mining and quarrying (excluding coal)	..	1,429	1,629	1,663	114·0	116·4
Public works contracting	..	..	3,474	2,965	3,926	85·4	113·0
General iron founding	..	..	3,107	3,865	3,497	124·4	112·6
Cocoa, chocolate, etc.	..	..	2,363	2,410	2,480	101·9	104·9
Chemicals, etc.	..	..	7,034	6,992	7,231	99·4	102·8
Cardboard boxes, paper bags, stationery, etc.	..	1,651	1,751	1,690	106·1	102·4
Tanning	..	..	2,859	2,743	2,914	95·9	101·9
Gas, water, and electricity supply‡	..	5,566	5,507	5,650	98·9	101·5
Local government services‡	..	..	10,880	10,603	10,955	97·5	100·7

* Other than tramway and omnibus service.
† Other than tailoring, dressmaking, millinery, boots and shoes, etc.
‡ In these and certain other industrial categories considerable numbers of workpeople are not covered by the insurance statistics, and complete figures might show somewhat different changes.

demand for certain products, application of labour-saving methods which enable the needs of the community to be supplied by a smaller number of workpeople, and the growth of demand for new products and services as the productive capacity of the community increases and its standard of living is raised. The effects of these tendencies upon the industrial structure of West Yorkshire may be examined by considering first those industries which have expanded during the last twelve years. The statistics given on pages 44 and 45 show the estimated numbers of insured workpeople aged 16 to 64 in employment in June 1923, June 1934, and June 1935 in thirteen West Yorkshire towns.[1] The industries are arranged in order, beginning with those showing the greatest expansion in 1935 compared with 1923.

Electrical engineering and electric wiring and contracting head the list, having the greatest rates of expansion. Between 1923 and 1935 the numbers they employed increased by nearly three times and two and a half times respectively. The total numbers they employed still remained small compared with other branches of industry. The greatest increase in

[1] The towns are the twelve chief centres mentioned earlier, together with Pontefract, which is added because of its importance in coal-mining. The numbers in employment are calculated by deducting the numbers unemployed from the estimated numbers insured. The 1923 figures compiled by the Ministry of Labour included persons over 64 years of age, but in the figures given above a correction has been made to ensure reasonable comparability.

numbers was in the distributive trades, which found employment for 21,000 more workpeople in 1935 than in 1923. With this increase is associated a considerably higher standard in the display of goods for sale, and improved service for customers. Tailoring provided work for 13,000 more workpeople in 1935 than eleven years earlier, the expansion being mainly in Leeds. Road transportation, including tramway and omnibus services, employed 6,000 more workpeople, while an almost similar increase took place in building.

A high rate of expansion is shown by laundries and dry cleaning, with an increase of about 3,000 workpeople; less laundry work is being done at home, while the same is true also of baking. Increases of over 2,000 took place in printing and publishing, and of about 1,600 in professional services. Substantial growth is shown by brickmaking, artificial silk, and manufacture of motor vehicles. The higher standard of living is reflected in the increased provision made for entertainments and sports, which show a rate of expansion of about 100 per cent. The rate of growth of hotel, public-house, restaurant, and boarding-house services was about 30 per cent. It may be noted that many of the expanded industries are engaged almost entirely in supplying the home market.

The contraction of certain industries has been more marked than the expansions. Corresponding statistics are given below for important branches of industry which show declines. It must be emphasized that they show the numbers in employment, and that, owing to the greater volume of unemployment in 1935 than in 1923, the declines would be less than those shown if comparisons were made of the numbers in employment together with persons out of work but considered as being attached to the different industries.[1] The rates of decline would therefore be reduced by further improvement in trade. Such improvements took place particularly in general engineering, woollen and worsted manufacture, and coal mining between 1934 and 1936, and the declines in these industries have consequently been reduced.

The outstanding change shown by the statistics is the heavy reduction since 1923 in the numbers employed in the woollen and worsted industry. This industry, together with the associated industry of textile dyeing and finishing, employed nearly 42,000 fewer insured workpeople in 1935 than in 1923. Decline in the export trade, together with reductions from the expansion of war-time and the early post-war years, were the chief factors. How severe has been the decline in this industry is indicated by the fact that it has counterbalanced the advances in employment made by the distributive trades, tailoring, building, and printing.

Other serious declines were experienced by coal-

---

[1] The statistics include persons on systematic short-time, but recorded as unemployed at the dates on which the statistics were compiled.

CONTRACTED INDUSTRIES

Industry	Numbers in Employment			Percentages in 1934 and 1935 compared with 1923 (= 100)	
	1923	1934	1935	1934	1935
Carpet manufacture..	5,075	4,915	4,987	96·8	98·3
Drink industries	2,903	3,217	2,666	110·8	91·8
General engineering..	38,878	30,295	33,345	77·9	85·8
Boot and shoe manufacture ..	3,510	2,933	2,881	83·5	82·1
Railway service (non-permanent)*	3,595	2,695	2,835	74·9	78·9
Commerce, banking, and insurance†	2,823	2,052	2,169	72·7	76·8
Woollen and worsted	158,670	112,285	120,882	70·8	76·2
Constructional engineering ..	1,014	959	728	94·6	71·8
Dressmaking and millinery ..	2,642	1,769	1,774	66·9	67·1
Textile dyeing and finishing ..	11,984	8,191	8,014	68·3	66·9
Woodworking‡	2,304	1,533	1,503	66·5	65·2
National government services† ..	2,868	1,832	1,832	63·9	63·9
Carriages, carts, etc.	1,061	622	601	58·6	56·6
Coal-mining	50,150	24,750§	27,000§	49·3	53·8
Leather goods manufacture ..	1,771	686	693	37·6	39·1
Railway carriages, wagons, and tramcar construction	2,576	907	1,002	35·2	38·9

* This group covers only a small fraction of workpeople in railway service.
† See footnote 3 on p. 45.   ‡ Other than furniture making.
§ Figure for November, a month of good season activity.

D

mining, the reduction in employment among insured persons being around 23,000, and by general engineering, with a reduction in 1935 of over 5,000 compared with 1923. The general causes of the decline in employment in coal-mining are well known—competition of oil and other fuels, more economical use of fuel, increase in the application of mechanized methods, and reduction in export, while West Yorkshire has also suffered from the greater competition from other districts.[1] General engineering, like coal-mining, has suffered from loss of foreign markets, but also from a tendency for certain branches of the industry to move to other parts of the country; for example, railway rolling stock formerly made in West Yorkshire for British railways is now more concentrated in the workshops of the companies in other districts. Mention may also be made of the leather industries—manufacture of boots and shoes and other leather goods—which record declines. As already indicated, the position of some of the declining industries was less unfavourable in 1936 than in 1935 owing to the effect of further recovery in reducing unemployment. Recently, therefore, the decline in some of the contracting industries has been checked or even reversed.

[1] Employment in British coal-mining was at an exceptionally high level in 1923, at the time of the Ruhr occupation. In June of that year in the 13 West Yorkshire towns the number of persons aged 16 to 64 who were unemployed was only 1,030, whereas in November 1935 the number of men out of work had increased about sevenfold to a total of 7,127.

VI

REVIEW OF CHIEF INDUSTRIES

In the preceding section statistics were given for about fifty different industries. Nine of these industries have been selected for more detailed study because of their outstanding importance or special interest. They are the wool and worsted, textile dyeing and finishing, tailoring, engineering, coalmining, printing and bookbinding, building, the distributive trades, road transportation.[1] Together, as already indicated, they cover about 70 per cent of the total number of insured persons in all industries in the twelve chief towns. It should not be overlooked, however, that, in addition to these industries, there are many branches, each employing a few thousand workpeople, which contribute greatly to the prosperity of the area, increasing its industrial stability and offering a wide range of occupations.

It is convenient to group the industries into localized and non-localized industries, the three industries mentioned last in the above list being

[1] Railway transportation is not included, as the statistics compiled by the Ministry of Labour cover only non-permanent workers, and this group is not sufficiently representative. Permanent railway workers are not included in the Unemployment Insurance Scheme, and comparable data are not available for them.

given in the second of these groups. The localized industries mainly give West Yorkshire its industrial character, and are not merely localized in the area but also tend to be concentrated in certain centres within the area. The distinction between localized and non-localized industries is not always sharp. Coal-mining is inevitably localized where the coal measures are found, but tailoring might be distributed in many centres, although in West Yorkshire it is highly concentrated in Leeds. At one time the woollen industry was widely distributed throughout the country but later became localized in a few districts, chiefly West Yorkshire. Some engineering is found in most towns, but the chief branches of the industry are localized. In recent years the drift of industry to the South of England has focused attention upon the causes of localization, and it is now recognized that few industries are so dependent upon the material resources of a district as to be permanently located there. The part played by the human factors of efficiency, initiative, and adaptability in meeting changing conditions is becoming increasingly important.

For each of the nine industries reviewed below, statistics for the country as a whole are given in Appendix II, as these are of interest for the purpose of comparison with the trends shown by the statistics for West Yorkshire.

(1) Localized Industries

Wool and Worsted

Wool and worsted textile manufacture, together with the associated dyeing and finishing industry and clothing manufacture, form the chief localized industrial group in West Yorkshire. This group offers a much greater field for the employment of labour than any other industry in the area. During the eighteenth and nineteenth centuries West Yorkshire became predominant in woollen and worsted manufacture compared with other parts of Great Britain. It is outside the scope of this review to examine the factors, including the coal and iron resources of the area, which enabled the industry to become concentrated in West Yorkshire. It may be noted, however, that modern developments of transportation and especially the distribution of electrical power have diminished the importance of localizing industries near to the coal mines and to supplies of iron and raw materials. Convenience in marketing the finished product has increased in importance. At the present time, therefore, the localization of the woollen and worsted industry is less dependent than formerly upon local products. It is based largely upon the presence of a large force of skilled workpeople, upon specialized markets for the sale of partly manufactured products, and upon other "economies" which firms in associated lines of production obtain from close proximity to one another. These are real advantages, but they are somewhat precarious, and it is significant that a branch of the textile industry—the manufacture of knitted goods and hosiery—which uses wool yarn extensively, has developed rapidly during recent years in the Midlands and not in West Yorkshire, although much yarn for this industry is spun in West Yorkshire.

Within West Yorkshire different towns tend to specialize in one or other branch of the woollen and worsted industry. The nature of this specialization is well summarized in the following passage from the *Survey of Textile Industries* prepared by the Committee on Industry and Trade.[1] "To a certain extent the woollen and worsted branches are concentrated in separate districts, though the separation is by no means complete. The worsted branch is located mainly in and around Bradford, Halifax, and Keighley—to the west and north, while the woollen branch is located mainly about Leeds, Batley, Dewsbury, and Morley—to the east and south. In Huddersfield both branches are carried on, some of the best worsteds for men's wear and some fine woollens being produced. The Colne Valley above Huddersfield specializes in cheaper kinds of woollen goods, while Dewsbury and Batley specialize mainly in still lower qualities in which shoddy plays a large part. Leeds produces a somewhat wide variety of woollen goods, together with

[1] P. 165.

a considerable amount of worsted yarns and cloth Bradford is the centre of wool combing and of the manufacture (together with Halifax) of worsted goods for women's wear, and is the principal commercial centre of the industry, though it is naturally more concerned with worsteds than with woollens."

The supremacy of West Yorkshire in the woollen and worsted industry of the country is shown by the Census statistics. At the time of the 1921 Census the total number of persons in the woollen and worsted industry in Great Britain was 259,692, and of these, over 206,000, or about 80 per cent, were in West Yorkshire.[1] Ten years later the total number of persons in the industry in Great Britian had fallen to 248,000, this decline being about 5 per cent. In West Yorkshire the number had fallen to 200,000, but the district maintained, or even slightly increased, its predominance relatively to other districts. The post-war decline has been largely due to difficulties experienced in markets abroad. These difficulties have resulted to a considerable extent, from the growing tendency for other countries to become more self-sufficient by increasing manufacture at home.[2]

[1] The figures include persons out of work at the time of the Census. They relate to the whole of the West Riding, but the industry is concentrated in West Yorkshire as defined in this review.

[2] A detailed review of industrial and commercial conditions is given in the section on wool in the *Survey of Textile Industries* by the Committee on Industry and Trade. See also a paper on

The table opposite gives statistics showing the trends of employment and unemployment in the industry during recent years. The statistics show a decline during the period from 1924 to 1936 of about 10 per cent in the number of insured adult workpeople in the industry in the twelve chief towns of West Yorkshire, while the decline during the same period in the numbers in employment was about 16 per cent. Unemployment shows wide variations from under 5 per cent in May 1924 to more than 27 per cent in May 1932 at the worst period of the depression.[1] A substantial recovery then began, and the relatively low unemployment percentages of 9·3 in November 1933 and 9·5 in November 1935 were recorded; the number of unemployed persons represented by these figures were still considerable, being around 12,000.

The industry employs considerably more women than men. In 1935 the number of insured adult male workers in the twelve chief towns of West Yorkshire was about 53,600, and the number of adult females was 79,000. The recovery years have seen a considerably greater proportionate reduction,

"The Distribution of Employment in the Wool Textile Industry of the West Riding of Yorkshire," by A. N. Shimmin (*Journal of Royal Statistical Society*, January 1926), and a paper read by George H. Wood before the Royal Statistical Society in February 1927, giving an index of employment activity in the industry.

[1] The situation in 1930 had been aggravated by a protracted industrial dispute about wages.

ESTIMATED NUMBERS OF INSURED PERSONS, AGED 18 TO 64, THE NUMBERS IN EMPLOYMENT, AND PERCENTAGES UNEMPLOYED IN THE WOOLLEN AND WORSTED INDUSTRY IN WEST YORKSHIRE TOWNS, 1924 AND 1928 TO 1936

Year	Estimated numbers of insured men and women*	Estimated numbers in employment in May of each year	Percentage of insured workpeople unemployed	
			May	*November*
1924	146,370	139,281	4·8	9·5
1928	141,200	128,822	8·8	14·7
1929	139,680	123,981	11·2	16·6
1930	142,640	112,220	21·3	25·5
1931	143,960	103,353	26·8	19·6
1932	140,180	102,065	27·2	18·2
1933	137,840	117,055	15·1	9·3
1934	136,430	112,956	17·2	13·0
1935	132,590	114,158	13·9	8·5
1936†	131,000	117,750	10·1	—

* Statistics for July.   † Provisional; official figures not available.

of unemployment among women than among men. Thus, in November 1935, when the percentage of unemployment among men and women together was 8·5, the percentage for men was about 13, but the percentage for women was only 5·5, or less than one-half of the men's rate. In pre-depression years and in the early years of the depression the difference was much smaller; for example, in November 1924 unemployment among men was about 11 per cent and among women nearly 9 per cent. The small percentage of unemployment among women in months of good seasonal activity during the recent recovery is illustrated by the fact that in various centres there has been a shortage of female labour, and a number of women and girls from other parts of the country have found jobs in West Yorkshire.

The number of juvenile workers in the industry is considerable. Insured youths and girls between the ages of fourteen and eighteen years numbered 17,490 in the twelve chief towns of West Yorkshire in July 1935, and formed a proportion of 13·2 per cent of the total number of insured workpeople. Except when the industry is suffering from considerable depression, unemployment among juvenile workers is small.

In addition to its unemployment insurance statistics the Ministry of Labour obtains returns each month from a large number of firms showing the total number of workpeople employed. These data pro-

INDEX FIGURES SHOWING CHANGES IN THE TOTAL NUMBER OF WORKPEOPLE EMPLOYED IN THE CHIEF CENTRES OF THE WOOLLEN AND WORSTED INDUSTRY IN WEST YORKSHIRE AT VARIOUS DATES. (JANUARY 1926 = 100)*

Section and District	May 1928	May 1932	May 1934	May 1935	May 1936
Woollen Section					
Huddersfield	93·5	83·8	91·0	90·2	98·6
Heavy Woollen District†	105·2	84·1	85·3	83·2	84·7
Leeds	108·0	83·2	104·3	95·7	102·7
Halifax and Calder Vale	95·0	88·9	92·2	89·9	99·2
Bradford	108·4	93·9	93·4	95·4	95·4
West Yorkshire	100·9	85·5	93·1	90·3	96·1
Worsted Section					
Bradford	98·9	84·8	84·0	89·0	89·4
Huddersfield	109·3	88·9	86·4	85·7	89·8
Halifax	95·8	80·8	74·0	77·2	81·2
Leeds	97·3	91·4	88·0	91·9	96·4
Keighley	103·4	91·0	89·0	87·6	91·1
Heavy Woollen District†	102·0	101·0	99·1	103·4	107·2
West Yorkshire	100·2	86·6	84·4	87·6	89·9

* The figures relate to the same firms at each date, and cover all wage earners irrespective of age, sex, or occupation.
† Dewsbury, Batley etc.

vide a basis for comparing changes during a period of years in each of the chief centres of the woollen and worsted sections of the industry. Index figures showing changes in recent years are tabulated on page 59. They are calculated from returns made by firms employing about 100,000 workpeople in May 1936, and are therefore fairly representative.

These statistics show declines in both the woollen and the worsted sections in recent years compared with the base period (January 1926), the decline being appreciably greater in the worsted than in the woollen section. Both sections show recovery since 1932, but the improvement has been greater in wool than in worsted. In the woollen section Leeds shows the best rate, and the heavy woollen district (Dewsbury, Batley, etc.) the worst. In the worsted section also Leeds is in a relatively favourable position, although the worsted section in the Dewsbury and Batley district shows the best level of employment, thus offsetting to some extent the decline in heavy woollen manufacture.

Textile Dyeing and Finishing

Some textile dyeing and finishing is found in each of the towns in which the woollen and worsted trades are established, but the most important centres are Bradford, Huddersfield, and Leeds. In these three towns were located over 73 per cent of the total number of insured workpeople in the industry in the twelve chief towns of West Yorkshire in July 1935. Bradford alone represented nearly one-half of the total.

The fortunes of the West Yorkshire textile dyeing and finishing industry are intimately associated with those of wool and worsted. The decline in wool and worsted is, therefore, reflected in a fall in employment in dyeing and finishing. This fall has been even greater than in wool and worsted, partly owing to measures of rationalization which have been applied in the industry. In July 1935 the estimated number of insured adult workpeople in the chief centres had fallen to 10,470, or about 73 per cent of the number in July 1924. As unemployment was considerably greater in the latter than in the former year, the numbers in employment in July 1935 show an even greater fall, the volume of employment being under 8,000, or only about 65 per cent of the 1924 level.

The worst years of the depression were 1930 and 1931, when the rate of unemployment was well over 40 per cent and sometimes exceeded 50 per cent, e.g., in May 1930. In 1930, in addition to the depression, employment was affected by a protracted dispute about wages in the woollen and worsted industry. Subsequent years show marked improvement, but in 1936 the rate of unemployment remained above 20 per cent, this being considerably higher than in 1924, and much greater than in most other industries in the district. Unemployment among women is

ESTIMATED NUMBERS OF INSURED PERSONS, AGED 18 TO 64, NUMBERS IN EMPLOYMENT, AND PERCENTAGES UNEMPLOYED IN THE TEXTILE DYEING AND FINISHING INDUSTRY IN WEST YORKSHIRE TOWNS, 1924 AND 1928 TO 1936

Year	Estimated numbers of insured men and women*	Estimated numbers in employment in May of each year	Percentage of insured workpeople unemployed	
			May	November
1924	14,370	12,286	14·5	15·0
1928	12,730	10,681	16·1	26·8
1929	12,220	8,887	27·3	23·2
1930	11,900	5,874	50·7	47·1
1931	11,260	5,736	49·1	42·9
1932	10,850	6,815	37·2	38·3
1933	11,230	8,173	27·2	24·3
1934	10,810	7,896	27·0	25·2
1935	10,470	7,933	24·2	23·6
1936†	10,200	7,700	24·7	—

* Statistics for July.   † Provisional.

relatively small, and therefore the percentages for men would be somewhat higher than those tabulated opposite for men and women together. Male workers, however, predominate in the industry, the proportion of female workers being only between 15 and 16 per cent of the total.

Statistics of the estimated numbers of insured adult workpeople, the numbers in employment, and percentages unemployed in this industry during recent years, are given in the table opposite.

Tailoring

The tailoring industry in West Yorkshire is noteworthy for its concentration in Leeds. In 1935 about 93 per cent of the industry was located there, the estimated number of insured adult workpeople in Leeds being 40,470 out of a total of 43,450 in the twelve chief towns. Huddersfield followed with 1,460 adult workpeople or only about 3·3 per cent of the total, while Bradford came next with few more than one-half the number in Huddersfield. The industry includes a wide variety of types of firms ranging from small workshops with a few workpeople to large undertakings numbering their employees by thousands.

The industry has enjoyed rapid expansion during post-war years, and in 1936 it employed over 40 per cent more workpeople than in 1924. The rate of expansion slowed down for a year or two during the depression, but it did not entirely cease. The industry has had the advantage of freedom from severe foreign competition and has benefited from the stimulus of rising standards of living, one expression of which has been a demand for an improved standard of dress, to which the industry has made a big contribution.

Tailoring is highly seasonal. This is clearly seen in the table opposite by comparing the percentages of unemployment in May with those in November. In the latter month unemployment was invariably very much greater than in May, sometimes being ten or more times as great. Often 3,000 to 5,000 more adults are unemployed in November than in May. Being a rapidly expanding industry, the rate of unemployment was so low at the peaks of seasonal activity as to represent a shortage of labour. Tailoring did not escape from the effects of the depression, for reduced purchasing power resulted in postponement of demand for new suits. Nevertheless, even in 1932—the worst year of the depression—the rate of unemployment during the busy season of May rose only to about 8 per cent, this being considerably below the rate in most other industries. Seasonal slackness, however, combined with the effects of the trade depression, resulted in an unemployment rate of 20 per cent in November of that year.

Over 70 per cent of the total number of workpeople in the industry are women and girls. The industry employs more than 10,000 juveniles. Nearly 20 per cent of the total number of insured

ESTIMATED NUMBERS OF INSURED PERSONS, AGED 18 TO 64, THE NUMBERS IN EMPLOYMENT, AND PERCENTAGES UNEMPLOYED IN THE TAILORING IN- DUSTRY IN WEST YORKSHIRE TOWNS, 1924 AND 1928 TO 1936

Year	Estimated numbers of insured men and women*	Estimated numbers in employment in May of each year†	Percentage of Insured Workpeople unemployed	
			May	November
1924	30,770	30,282	1·6	11·2
1928	35,430	35,095	0·9	12·2
1929	35,220	34,767	1·3	9·5
1930	35,930	34,264	4·6	18·3
1931	38,300	36,485	4·7	16·2
1932	39,860	36,634	8·1	20·3
1933	41,160	39,372	4·3	13·2
1934	41,760	40,271	3·6	13·1
1935	43,450	41,982	3·4	11·0
1936‡	44,500	43,440	2·4	—

* Statistics for July.
† The numbers would be considerably smaller in November owing to the heavier unemployment in that month.
‡ Provisional; official figures not available.

E

workpeople in July 1935 were boys and girls between fourteen and eighteen years of age. There is, indeed, a shortage of juvenile labour in Leeds, and considerable numbers are recruited from a distance.

The statistics of insured adults in the industry and of employment and unemployment among such persons are given in the preceding table.

Engineering[1]

The term "engineering" covers a large number of distinct branches of industry, and many of these branches are established in West Yorkshire. Heavy engineering preponderates, though a development of the lighter branches is gradually taking place, facilitated by the progress of modern transportation. This preponderance of heavy engineering explains why, as is indicated in Section ix, the increase in the number of women relatively to men has been smaller in West Yorkshire than in those parts of the country in which the light branches of the industry are more important. General engineering is the preponderating branch in West Yorkshire, employing considerably more than double the number of workpeople in electrical engineering, constructional engineering, and construction and repair of motor vehicles, cycles and aircraft together. The present section deals mainly with general engineering, which itself covers a wide range of

[1] In writing this section the results of investigations made by R. K. Bacon have been used.

products, but comparisons are made between this and the other main branches of the industry.

Leeds is the chief engineering centre in West Yorkshire, with nearly 13,000 insured workers, or more than one-third of the total in the whole area. Its products include locomotives, both steam and Diesel, textile machinery, machine tools, gas plant, drop forgings and pressings, agricultural machinery, printing machinery, pumping machinery, water meters, boilers, road rollers, light armaments, concrete mixers, and clay-working machinery. Huddersfield follows, with more than 5,000 insured workpeople. It has the largest gear-making industry in the world, and is famous for its valves, pressure gauges, boiler mountings and other boiler-house instruments; its products also include textile machinery, electric motors, and commercial motor vehicles.

Bradford, with over 4,000 insured workers, manufactures power transmission and other equipment particularly for woollen and worsted mills, also boilers, piston rings, girders, lifts, motor cars, and a wide range of electrical goods. Keighley also has more than 4,000 insured workers; its products include textile machinery of all kinds, machine tools, laundry and agricultural machinery, gas, oil, and Diesel engines, lifts, cranes, stamping machinery, and brickmaking machinery. Halifax, with over 3,500 insured workpeople, is one of the chief centres in the country for the manufacture of machine tools, lathes, radial drills, boring, grinding, and woodworking machinery; spindles are made, and the manufacture of cash registers and time recorders is increasing. Wakefield, with about 2,250 insured workpeople, manufactures railway wagons, passenger and goods road vehicle bodies, boilers, colliery plant, fuel economizers, and sheet-metal working machinery.

The preceding paragraphs have indicated the wide variety of branches and products of the industry. The post-war period has been one of rapid change both in types of product and in methods of production, and the problem of the industry has been, and continues to be, adaptation to technical and other changes. Considerable stresses have resulted from the rapidity of the changes. Among the important developments have been the increasing use of electrically driven plant in place of steam, and the progress of internal combustion engines, and particularly the competition of the road motor vehicle with the railway locomotive. West Yorkshire has not become a great centre for motor car manufacture, but various components are produced, including steel pressings, stampings and forgings, pistons, piston rings, and gears. It has lost considerably from decline in the export trade in locomotives, and from the policy of the railway companies to manufacture locomotives and other rolling-stock in their own engineering shops, located in other parts of the country, instead of giving out large contracts to engineering firms. Leeds in particular has suffered seriously from this transference and from the decline in exports. Other branches of heavy engineering, together with the manufacture of textile machinery, have also suffered decline during post-war years. Directly and indirectly the district is, however, benefiting somewhat from the Government's programme of armament manufacture, while the building boom has led to increased production of clay-working machines (for brick and tile making) and concrete mixers.

Statistics are tabulated on page 70 showing, for the four chief branches of engineering located in West Yorkshire, the numbers of insured persons aged sixteen to sixty-four years in the four chief centres —Leeds, Huddersfield, Bradford, and Halifax—together with the average numbers and percentages unemployed. The figures cover the worst year of the depression—1932—and the subsequent period of recovery. They show the predominant position of general engineering, which, however, with constructional engineering, has suffered from much higher rates of unemployment than electrical engineering and construction and repairs of motor vehicles, cycles, and aircraft.

For general engineering, statistics are given on page 72 for the period from 1924 to 1936. They cover the twelve chief towns of West Yorkshire and relate only to men; the general trends are not affected considerably by the relatively small number of women and juvenile workers in the industry. In the

ESTIMATED NUMBERS OF INSURED PERSONS,
AVERAGE NUMBERS AND PERCENTAGES OF
UNEMPLOYMENT IN CERTAIN BRANCHES OF
ENGINEERING IN FOUR WEST YORKSHIRE
TOWNS, 1932 TO 1936*

	GENERAL ENGINEERING		
	Estimated numbers	*Unemployment*	
Year	*of insured persons*	*Average numbers*	*Percentage*
1932	26,080	8,148	31·2
1933	24,430	6,909	28·3
1934	24,560	3,834	15·6
1935	26,150	2,782	10·6
1936	—	2,392	—
	ELECTRICAL ENGINEERING		
1932	2,360	200	8·5
1933	2,540	192	7·6
1934	2,450	173	7·1
1935	2,670	125	4·7
1936	—	94	—
	CONSTRUCTIONAL ENGINEERING		
1932	960	284	29·6
1933	870	247	28·4
1934	1,000	164	16·4
1935	750	132	17·6
1936	—	80	—
	CONSTRUCTION AND REPAIR OF MOTOR VEHICLES, CYCLES, AND AIRCRAFT		
1932	4,170	393	9·4
1933	4,160	255	6·1
1934	4,330	173	4·0
1935	3,990	292	7·3
1936	—	283	—

* The estimated numbers of insured persons are for July of
each year. The unemployment figures are averages calculated
from the returns for a date in January, April, July, and
October of each year except 1936, which cover January and
April only.

early part of the period the industry was still suffering from the considerable expansion in the number of workpeople during the war. The statistics show a decline of about 12 per cent in the number of insured men between 1924 and 1936; the decline came to an end in 1933 when trade began to improve. The numbers in employment in May 1936 were about 9 per cent fewer than May 1924. Unemployment fell from a total of about 11,000 men in May 1931 and May 1932 to only 2,509 in May 1936, while the rates of unemployment fell from more than 33 per cent in 1932 to around 10 or 11 per cent in 1935. This level was almost the same as that in 1924 and the spring of 1929, but the number in the industry was smaller by several thousand. In May 1936 the rate of unemployment was lower than at any other period covered by the table. During the depression general engineering in West Yorkshire suffered more severely from unemployment than the industry in the country as a whole, but it has enjoyed a better rate of recovery.

Coal Mining[1]

The West Yorkshire coalfield is geologically continuous with the mining areas of South Yorkshire, Nottinghamshire, and North Derbyshire, and, from the geological standpoint, the boundaries between

[1] In the preparation of this section use has been made of a memorandum prepared by W. Prest, Economics Department, St. Andrews University.

ESTIMATED NUMBERS OF INSURED MEN, THE NUMBERS IN EMPLOYMENT AND PERCENTAGES UNEMPLOYED IN GENERAL ENGINEERING IN WEST YORKSHIRE, 1924 AND 1928 TO 1936

Year	Estimated numbers of insured men*	Estimated numbers in employment in May of each year	Percentages of insured men unemployed	
			May	November
1924	38,610	34,502	10·6	11·7
1928	34,670	30,861	10·9	14·0
1929	34,980	31,020	11·3	16·3
1930	34,480	26,615	22·8	31·8
1931	33,320	22,286	33·1	30·8
1932	32,540	21,603	33·6	33·9
1933	31,340	22,054	29·6	21·9
1934	31,590	26,779	15·2	13·8
1935	32,850	29,189	11·1	10·2
1936†	34,000	31,500	7·4	—

* Figures for July.   † Provisional; official figures not available.

these areas are quite arbitrary. Nevertheless, in its organization for certain administrative purposes and for wage negotiations, and in some economic aspects, West Yorkshire constitutes a separate mining area. Within this area the industry is mainly concentrated to the east of the line from Leeds to Wakefield, and about three-quarters of the total output is raised in this eastern section. The three employment exchange areas of Castleford, Pontefract, and Wakefield, representing the eastern section, alone cover about 28,000 out of a total of 34,350 insured workpeople in thirteen important West Yorkshire areas for which statistics are available. West of the Leeds–Wakefield line the seams are thinner and nearer to the surface than in the east; in the hills of the western section outcrops of coal are frequent. The total number of mines is nearly 120, the size varying considerably. The large collieries are mainly in the eastern section.

The coal produced is primarily suitable for household and manufacturing purposes; the amount of gas, coking, and steam coal is relatively small. The manufacturing industries and concentration of population in West Yorkshire provide the chief market, although the eastern section exports coal from the Humber to Northern and Central Europe. Recently the annual output of saleable coal has been about 11 million tons. This compares with an average annual production of 14¾ million tons during the period 1909–13. The peak of production was in

1913. Since the war the best period was 1923–24,[1] but this was followed by a serious decline during the next four years, and by a further serious decline during the great depression, and subsequent recovery in coal-mining has only been slight. The post-war decline in West Yorkshire has been relatively somewhat greater than in Yorkshire as a whole or in Great Britain as a whole. In the western section of the area the decline has been more marked than in the east.

Smaller sales in foreign markets have been one cause of the industry's difficulties. Recently exports from the Humber have been a little over three million tons annually compared with almost three times as much in 1913. More important, however, is the fall in home market sales. This has been due partly to trade depression since 1929, but partly also to the increasing adoption of methods of fuel economy and the use of oil, while competition of South Yorkshire coal has also been a factor.

The labour force is probably not far short of 50,000, but the number on the colliery books is only about 45,000 workpeople. In a sense these workpeople are in employment, but, owing to systematic short-time working, they are subject to serious under-employment, even during the periods of greatest seasonal activity. The income of large numbers of miners consists of their earnings for

[1] In 1923 the industry enjoyed great temporary prosperity at the time of the Ruhr occupation.

several days' work each week and unemployment benefit for the remainder of the week. Men in receipt of benefit for days when they are not working owing to systematic short time are recorded by the Ministry of Labour as "temporarily stopped," and are included in the unemployed totals.[1] Thus many men on the colliery books are reckoned among the unemployed in the statistics compiled by the Ministry of Labour. The numbers on the colliery books are useful, however, in indicating general trends. The average numbers of persons on the colliery books in West Yorkshire during recent years are as follows[2]:

1923	70,889	1930	52,341
1924	72,744	1931	51,037
1925	68,662	1932	49,353
1927*	64,442	1933	44,765
1928	56,714	1934	44,245
1929	53,588	1935	43,500†

* The year 1926 is omitted as figures for that year are of little value in consequence of the protracted stoppage of the industry during that year.   † Provisional.

These figures show a decline of nearly 40 per cent between 1923 and 1935. Some indication of under-employment among those on the colliery books is given by the number of days annually on which

[1] Except in good years and in periods of seasonal activity the number temporarily stopped is greater than the number wholly unemployed. The "temporarily stopped" category may include persons not working systematic short time, e.g. men stopped because of accidents, breakdowns, etc.

[2] The 1913 figure was 63,826.

coal was wound at the pits. In 1934 the average number was only 201·66, while during the last nine years the highest average in any year was 223·9 days in 1929.[1]

The trends of employment and unemployment among men in the industry as shown by the Ministry of Labour's statistics are tabulated on page 78. The statistics for women are not given, as the general trends are not appreciably affected by the relatively few women in the industry. The number of insured boys and youths, fourteen to eighteen years of age, was about 2,660 in July 1935, or roughly about 7·5 per cent of the total number of insured workpeople in the industry; these also are not included in the table. The statistics show that the number of insured men was about 38 per cent less in 1936 than in 1924. The fall in the numbers in employment was considerably greater, being about 48 per cent between November 1924 and November 1935; over 49,000 were employed in November 1924, but fewer than 26,000 eleven years later.

Notwithstanding the great decline in the number of insured workers, unemployment among those who remained was exceptionally high throughout the whole period from 1928 onwards. This is in sharp contrast with the very low percentage of

[1] These averages do not give a very accurate indication of under-employment, as they are unduly affected by the figures for very small collieries which only work for a few months of the year, mainly when seasonal and cyclical trade conditions are favourable.

unemployment in 1924. The worst unemployment at the dates covered by the table was in May 1933, when the percentage was 57·2. At this time 21,000 miners, or considerably more than half the number of insured men, were out of work, though many of these were only "temporarily stopped." The general trade revival brought some relief to the industry after 1934, but recent percentages of unemployment indicate a persistent state of depression in the industry, and in November 1935 there were still more than 7,000 West Yorkshire miners unemployed. The rates of unemployment among West Yorkshire coal miners have been greater during recent years than among coal miners in Britain as a whole.

Improvements in technique have caused output to decline less rapidly than employment, with the result that there has been a distinct improvement in production per head. Since 1924 the decline in total output has been about 28 per cent, but annual output per head has increased by about 17 per cent. This is due partly to increase in the proportion of total output cut by machinery, which rose in West Yorkshire from about 25 per cent in 1924 to 43 per cent in 1934,[1] although the increased proportion, has resulted more from decline in hand-cut tonnage than increase in machine-cut tonnage. There has been some increase in the number of conveyors and other forms of mechanization, the effect of which on production has been more significant than that

[1] Annual Reports of the Secretary of Mines.

ESTIMATED NUMBERS OF INSURED MEN, THE NUMBERS IN EMPLOYMENT, AND PERCENTAGES UNEMPLOYED IN THE COAL MINING INDUSTRY IN WEST YORKSHIRE, 1924 AND 1928 TO 1936*

Year	Estimated numbers of insured men‡	Estimated numbers in employment in November of each year‡	Percentages of insured men employed	
			May	November
1924	51,460	49,798	1·6	3·2
1928	42,920	32,063	20·7	25·3
1929	40,480	32,683	26·2	19·8
1930	38,970	30,757	27·8	21·1
1931	38,250	25,415	25·5	33·6
1932	37,210	21,329	32·4	42·7
1933	36,810	23,622	57·2	35·8
1934	33,990	23,558	39·3	30·7
1935	32,970	25,843	38·1	21·6
1936§	31,500	—	28·7	—

* These statistics cover thirteen areas, namely the twelve towns upon which most of the statistics in this review are based, together with Pontefract. These represent a smaller area than that covered by the preceding statistics of persons on the colliery books.   † Statistics for July.

‡ The numbers would be considerably smaller in May owing to the heavy seasonal unemployment in that month. Also, as the trend of the numbers insured is downward, the estimated numbers in employment in November are somewhat too high, being calculated by deducting the numbers in unemployment in November from the estimated numbers insured in July. Similarly the unemployed percentages for May are slightly too high and those for November too low. These last two comments also apply to certain other tables in this study where the numbers insured in an industry have fallen considerably. The effect is the reverse in an industry where the numbers insured have risen.   § Provisional; unofficial estimate.

of increase in cutting machinery. Another factor affecting output has been the tendency during the prolonged depression to abandon the more difficult workings.

Printing and Bookbinding

As already seen, printing and bookbinding is one of the expanding industries of West Yorkshire. It is also very definitely localized within the area, with Leeds and Bradford as the two centres of importance. Thus in July 1935 out of a total of 11,720 insured persons aged 16 to 64 in this industry in the twelve largest towns in the area, 7,130 or 60·8 per cent, were in Leeds, and 2,650, or 22·6 per cent, were in Bradford. Thus the remaining ten towns represented less than one-fifth of the industry.

During the twelve years from 1924 to 1936 the number of insured adults aged 18 to 64 in the industry increased by more than 30 per cent in the twelve chief towns of the area. During the same period the corresponding numbers in employment rose from about 8,000 to over 10,000, a rise of more than 25 per cent. In July 1935 the 3,840 insured women in the industry represented about 35 per cent of the total number of insured adults (10,970). At the same date the number of insured juveniles aged 14 to 17, was 1,930.

In pre-depression years 1924, 1928, and 1929 there was little unemployment in the industry, the percentages for the months of May and November of these years averaging under 4½. At the worst period of the depression the unemployment rate had almost trebled. Since 1933 there has been a marked improvement, but even in 1934 and 1935 the unemployment percentages remained more than double those of the pre-depression years. The November percentages show no great difference from those for May.

The statistics upon which the above review is based are given in the table opposite.

(2) Non-localized Industries

Building[1]

The building industry is of special interest in view of the important part which it has played in the recent trade recovery. The maintenance of a high level of building activity in the future is desirable both because of its importance in sustaining recovery, and of the need for reconstructing considerable parts of the industrial centres of West Yorkshire, which were built before modern ideas of town planning, housing, and factory designing had been evolved. Slum clearance, which is already making considerable progress, is one aspect of the problem, but there is also much scope for improvement of factory buildings.

Building workers are employed in each town in numbers which are very roughly proportionate to the size of the town. Building is predominantly a man's

[1] This section is based in part upon notes prepared by J. N. Reedman, now on the staff of the University of Johannesburg.

ESTIMATED NUMBERS OF INSURED PERSONS, AGED 18 TO 64, THE NUMBERS IN EMPLOYMENT, AND PERCENTAGES UNEMPLOYED IN THE PRINTING INDUSTRY IN WEST YORKSHIRE TOWNS. 1924 AND 1928 TO 1936

Year	Estimated numbers of insured men and women*	Estimated numbers in employment in May of each year	Percentage of insured workpeople unemployed	
			May	November
1924	8,370	8,010	4·3	3·5
1928	9,780	9,368	4·2	4·3
1929	9,520	9,125	4·1	5·1
1930	9,680	8,935	7·7	9·3
1931	9,610	8,484	11·7	12·6
1932	10,240	8,945	12·6	10·2
1933	10,730	9,498	11·5	9·4
1934	10,730	9,583	10·7	9·3
1935	10,970	9,832	10·4	9·7
1936†	11,250	10,125	9·9	—

* Statistics for July

† Provisional; official figures not available.

F

industry; very few women are employed, and the number of juveniles is relatively small. In order, therefore, to examine the trends of employment and unemployment in this industry, it is only necessary to review the statistics for men, i.e. males of 18 years or over. These statistics are tabulated opposite, the figures being totals obtained by combining together the data for the twelve chief towns of the area.

These statistics show that during the twelve years from 1924 to 1936 the number of insured men increased by about 30 per cent, most of the increase being between 1924 and 1928, and between 1933 and 1935. The increase in the numbers in employment was smaller, as unemployment in recent years has been considerably greater than in 1924. The figures of the numbers in employment are for May of each year, this being a period of good employment in an industry which is subject to heavy seasonal unemployment during winter months, owing largely to the effect of bad weather on outside work. In 1932—the worst year of the depression —the number in employment in May was nearly 3,000 less than in the pre-depression year 1928. During the next two years there was a rapid increase followed by a slight rise between 1934 and 1935, and a considerable rise in the following year, so that in May 1936 over 6,500 more men were in employment than four years earlier.

The percentage of unemployment was lowest in 1924, being only 5·1 per cent in May and 8 per

ESTIMATED NUMBERS OF INSURED MEN, THE NUMBERS IN EMPLOYMENT, AND PERCENTAGES UNEMPLOYED IN THE BUILDING INDUSTRY IN WEST YORK-SHIRE TOWNS, 1924 AND 1928 TO 1936

Year	Estimated numbers of insured men*	Estimated numbers in employment in May of each year†	Percentage of insured workmen unemployed	
			May	November
1924	19,760	18,754	5·1	8·0
1928	21,850	19,849	13·1	20·0
1929	21,500	19,069	10·6	21·4
1930	22,710	18,478	18·7	29·8
1931	22,920	17,851	22·1	24·4
1932	23,430	16,875	28·0	34·8
1933	23,520	18,950	20·0	22·3
1934	24,920	21,444	14·0	20·3
1935	25,810	21,862	15·3	19·5
1936‡	26,500	23,498	11·3	—

* Figures for July of each year.

† These figures are calculated by deducting the number of men unemployed in May of each year from the estimated number of insured men in July. Though only approximations, the figures give a good indication of the trend of employment.   ‡ Provisional; official figures not available.

cent in November. In the pre-depression years 1928 and 1929 the percentages were about 2 to 2½ times those in 1924, while in November 1932 unemployment approached 35 per cent, or more than one out of every three workmen. The year 1933 showed marked improvement, while in 1934, 1935, and 1936 the unemployment percentages had fallen nearly to the pre-depression level in 1928 and 1929. It is noteworthy that, throughout the period from 1928 to 1934 the unemployment percentage in November never fell below 20, or one in five, while even in 1935 it was only slightly lower.

Distributive Trades

As already indicated, the distributive trades show a greater increase during the last twelve years in the numbers employed than any other industry in West Yorkshire. This tendency, which corresponds to that in Great Britain as a whole, has resulted from the need to provide increased facilities for the sale of goods now produced in such large quantities by the efficient processes of modern industry. In 1936 over 60,000 insured adult workpeople were employed in the distributive trades in the twelve chief towns of West Yorkshire. At that date the number was 45 per cent greater than in 1924, while the number of men and women in employment was 36 per cent greater. After 1932 the rate of expansion in the numbers of insured workpeople was much smaller than during the period from 1924 to 1932.

During the worst years of the depression the percentages of unemployment among insured adults in May and November ranged from 11 to nearly 13 per cent. These rates, though much higher than in pre-depression years, were low compared with those in many other industries. Since the depression the rates of unemployment in the distributive trades have remained considerably above those in the years 1924, 1928, and 1929. From seasonal causes unemployment is generally somewhat greater in November than in May. The statistics upon which these conclusions are based are given in the table on page 86.

The expansion since 1932 in the number of insured workpeople has been limited to adult males; the number of insured women remained almost stationary during this period, while the number of juveniles aged 16 to 18 years declined appreciably. The rate of unemployment among women was considerably lower than that among men throughout the period from 1924 to 1936. The following table shows the numbers and proportions of insured men, women, boys aged 16 to 18 years, and girls aged 16 to 18 years, in 1928, 1932, and 1935.

Category	1928		1932		1935*	
	Number	Percentage	Number	Percentage	Number	Percentage
Men	31,440	59·0	37,530	57·4	40,080	61·0
Women ..	16,100	30·2	20,830	31·9	20,610	31·4
Boys†	3,390	6·4	4,010	6·1	2,650	4·0
Girls† ..	2,350	4·4	2,990	4·6	2,370	3·6
Total ..	53,280	100·0	65,360	100·0	65,710	100·0

* Statistics for July.   † Aged 16 to 18 years.

ESTIMATED NUMBERS OF INSURED PERSONS, AGED 18 TO 64, THE NUMBERS IN EMPLOYMENT, AND PERCENTAGES UNEMPLOYED IN THE DISTRIBUTIVE TRADES IN WEST YORKSHIRE TOWNS, 1924 AND 1928 TO 1936

Year	Estimated numbers of insured men and women*	Estimated numbers in employment in May of each year	Percentage of insured workpeople unemployed	
			May	November
1924	42,060	40,825	2·9	4·6
1928	47,540	45,418	4·5	5·5
1929	50,160	47,831	4·6	6·6
1930	51,320	46,884	8·6	11·3
1931	55,960	49,881	10·9	12·8
1932	58,360	51,591	11·6	12·7
1933	59,620	52,945	11·2	11·0
1934	60,370	54,763	9·3	10·4
1935	60,690	54,957	9·4	9·7
1936†	61,000	55,700	8·7	—

* Statistics for July.   † Provisional; official figures not available.

Statistics for some of the chief branches of the distributive trades are given in the Census returns, and these are summarized for the year 1931 in the table on page 88, which also indicates the changes between 1921 and 1931 in the numbers employed.[1] The statistics include large numbers of persons not covered by the unemployment insurance system. Also, the area covered by these data is considerably larger than West Yorkshire, as the Census volumes do not enable statistics to be compiled for West Yorkshire alone. The figures represent the West Riding of Yorkshire less the five chief centres outside West Yorkshire—Barnsley, Doncaster, Rotherham, Sheffield, and York. The relationships and trends shown are, however, reasonably representative for West Yorkshire.

The statistics show rapid growth between 1921 and 1931 in the numbers employed in most branches of the distributive trades. The greatest increase was in the sugar confectionery trade, which more than doubled. The growth in numbers in coal, meat, furniture, and stationery and book distribution ranged from 33 per cent to nearly 47 per cent; decline was shown in the numbers employed in the sale of boots and shoes, while the numbers in clothing distribution remained almost unchanged. Wide range is shown in the proportion of females in the different branches, from nearly 70 per cent in

[1] The statistics on which this table is based were extracted from the Census returns by W. Prest.

CENSUS STATISTICS SHOWING NUMBERS EMPLOYED IN CERTAIN BRANCHES OF THE DISTRIBUTIVE TRADES IN 1931, AND COMPARISONS WITH 1921

Branch	Numbers employed in wholesale and retail trade in 1931	Percentages of Females to Total		Percentage of persons in wholesale trade to total in 1931	Percentage increase (+) or decrease (−) in total numbers in 1931 compared with 1921
		1921	1931		
Coal	5,184	4·94	4·80	—	+ 33·4
Sugar confectionery ..	3,797	63·51	69·98	9·22	+ 116·5
Grocery, etc. ..	15,786	32·12	24·56	10·54	+ 10·7
Meat	9,123	11·15	6·94	3·32	+ 38·5
Vegetables and fruit ..	5,758	22·97	16·29	21·83	+ 17·9
Clothing	26,332	37·83	42·78	44·23	− 0·8
Boots and shoes ..	2,260	39·80	45·84	8·36	− 7·9
Furniture	3,267	24·26	23·14	—	+ 46·8
Stationery and books ..	4,622	35·86	29·66	24·66	+ 33·4
Mixed businesses*	17,318	24·77	25·83	—	+ 21·8

* Including departmental stores.

sugar confectionery to under 5 per cent in coal and 7 per cent in meat. Wide variation is also shown in the proportion of persons in wholesale trade; it is smallest, and therefore the retail side is greatest in the meat trade, and is also small in the boot and shoe, sugar confectionery, and grocery trades.

Road Transportation

Road transportation includes regular tramway and omnibus services as well as other transportation of passengers, cartage and haulage of goods by road, and motor garage services. It is not localized, although more than 93 per cent of insured work-people in the twelve largest towns of West Yorkshire are registered in Leeds, Bradford, Wakefield, Huddersfield, Halifax, and Dewsbury. Its employees are predominantly men. Thus in July 1935 out of a total of 13,350 insured persons, 12,780 were men, while women numbered only 310, and juveniles of 16 to 18 years of age only 260, mainly boys.[1] In order, therefore, to consider the state of employment and unemployment in the industry a review of the statistics for men is quite adequate.

The industry has expanded rapidly throughout the post-war period and has had a relatively low rate of unemployment even during the depression. The number of insured men in West Yorkshire towns more than doubled between 1924 and 1936,

---

[1] In some previous years the number of these juveniles was somewhat higher.

ESTIMATED NUMBERS OF INSURED MEN, AGED 18 TO 64, THE NUMBERS IN EMPLOYMENT AND PERCENTAGES UNEMPLOYED IN ROAD TRANSPORT SERVICES IN WEST YORKSHIRE TOWNS, 1924 AND 1928 TO 1936

Year	Estimated numbers of insured men*	Estimated numbers in employment in May of each year	Percentage of insured men unemployed	
			May	November
1924	6,310	6,110	8·3	8·1
1928	9,550	8,861	7·2	8·8
1929	9,350	8,772	6·2	9·5
1930	10,720	9,726	9·3	12·3
1931	11,230	9,946	11·4	13·9
1932	11,890	10,397	12·6	15·2
1933	11,330	9,709	14·3	13·9
1934	12,040	10,608	11·9	12·7
1935	12,780	11,315	11·5	10·6
1936†	13,500	12,287	9·0	—

* Statistics for July.   † Provisional; official figures not available.

the total in the latter year being about 13,500, while the number in employment in May 1936 was approximately double that in May 1924. Expansion was interrupted by the depression, but was resumed during 1934. Before the depression, unemployment among insured men was around 8 per cent. In November 1932 it was 15·2, or almost double the pre-depression level. Three and a half years later it had fallen to 9·0, i.e. slightly above the rate before the depression. Seasonal factors are responsible for a higher rate of unemployment in November than in May, but the difference is not great.

The statistics upon which the above paragraph is based are given in the preceding table.

VII

THE AGE FACTOR IN UNEMPLOYMENT

INFORMATION about the age distribution of the unemployed is of value especially in considering their prospects of obtaining work, and in the selection of persons for training or transfer to other districts. It is also useful in connection with the organization of occupational and recreational activities for the unemployed. Quite different methods are often necessary for younger and for older persons.

Here attention is directed to the age distribution of unemployed adults (over 18 years of age), while, owing to its special interest, a separate chapter of this review is devoted to juvenile employment and unemployment. The statistics tabulated below show the numbers of unemployed men and women in different age groups in West Yorkshire at the beginning of November 1935, together with the percentages for West Yorkshire and for the whole country. Among unemployed men in West Yorkshire towns 42 per cent were over 45 years of age, this being a distinctly higher percentage than in the country as a whole. The prospect of these men being reabsorbed into industry in large numbers is considerably smaller than that of the younger men. The greatest number was between the ages of 25 and 34, while slightly over 20 per cent are shown

UNEMPLOYMENT BY AGE GROUPS AT NOVEMBER 4, 1935

Age group (years)	MEN			WOMEN		
	Number Unemployed	*Percentage*		*Number Unemployed*	*Percentage*	
		West Yorkshire	*Whole Country*		*West Yorkshire*	*Whole Country*
18–80	1,696	3·3	5·0	816	6·9	13·4
21–24	5,486	10·6	12·9	1,921	16·3	20·2
25–34	12,318	23·9	25·4	3,412	28·9	27·5
35–44	10,402	20·2	19·7	2,681	22·7	18·1
45–54	10,402	20·2	18·6	1,848	15·6	12·9
55–59	5,994	11·6	9·9	708	6·0	4·8
60–64	5,154	10·0	8·2	422	3·6	3·0
65 and over	88	0·2	0·3	2	0·0	0·1

in each of the three higher ten-year age groups. The West Yorkshire percentages for the younger men were lower than those for the whole country.

Among women under 25 years of age the West Yorkshire percentages are also considerably below those for the country as a whole. Above this age, however, the statistics show the position of West Yorkshire to be less favourable than that in the whole country. Over the age of 45, and especially between the ages of 55 and 64, the women's percentages are considerably smaller than those of men, this being due to the fact that the older women withdraw in large numbers from the labour market, whereas the men continue to demand employment. On the other hand, the percentages among young women are higher than those among young men. The industrial life of women is more concentrated than that of men.

The statistics upon which these statements are based are given in the preceding table.

VIII

DURATION OF UNEMPLOYMENT

THE burden of unemployment largely varies with the length of time a person is out of work. Short periods of unemployment extending over a few weeks, with reasonable prospects of soon obtaining a new job, do not present as great economic and social difficulties as a prolonged period extending for months or even years. Short periods involve much less deterioration of skill and aptitude for work, and have much less effect upon the workers' morale than extended periods of unemployment.

Statistics are tabulated on page 97 showing for the twelve chief towns of West Yorkshire the length of unemployment, in various periods from less than four weeks to five years or more, experienced by persons out of work in November 1935. The table shows that more than 20,000 persons had been unemployed for three months or more. Those who had been without jobs for a year or more numbered 9,428, while of these no less than 2,818 had been out of work continuously for three years or more. Nearly a quarter of those whose unemployment had continued throughout three years or more were in the coal-mining centre of Castleford, and more than 40 per cent were in Leeds.

The statistics show separately the duration of

unemployment for men, women, young men and boys, and young women and girls. Men only were affected in large numbers by prolonged unemployment. Over 96 per cent of the total numbers unemployed for a year or more were men. Few women were unemployed except for short periods, the total number unemployed for six months or more being quite small, while prolonged unemployment among juveniles was negligible. Most of the unemployment among young men and boys was between the ages of eighteen and twenty. This is no doubt due in part to the higher wages which must be paid as the age of youths increases, and indicates the existence of a certain number of blind-alley occupations.

It should be noted that the figures considerably understate the amount of prolonged unemployment. For example, if a man, after several years of unemployment, gets a job for a few weeks and then becomes unemployed again he is shown as having been unemployed for only a short period. In order to obtain a complete view of the duration of unemployment statistics should show not only the length of the latest period of continuous unemployment, but also the total amount of unemployment incurred during, for example, the last three months, six months, twelve months, two years, etc. These latter data are not available.

LENGTH OF LATEST PERIOD OF REGISTERED UNEMPLOYMENT OF PERSONS AGED 16 TO 64 YEARS IN WEST YORKSHIRE TOWNS AT NOVEMBER 25, 1935*

	Men aged 21–64 years	Young men and boys aged 16–20 years	Women aged 21–64 years	Young women and girls aged 16–20 years	Totals
5 years or more	639	—	11	—	650
4 years and under 5 years	913	—	12	—	925
3 years and under 4 years	1,218	—	25	—	1,243
2 years and under 3 years	2,097	5	51	—	2,153
1 year and under 2 years	4,200	35	221	1	4,457
9 months and under 1 year	2,140	33	151	5	2,329
6 months and under 9 months ..	2,618	56	299	4	2,977
3 months and under 6 months ..	4,691	142	670	28	5,531
2 months and under 3 months ..	3,533	161	604	21	4,319
4 weeks and under 8 weeks ..	3,768	195	629	54	4,646
Less than 4 weeks	6,530	478	1,035	106	8,149

* The statistics tabulated cover persons applying for insurance benefit and unemployment allowances who were on the register at the date stated; they also include a small number of juveniles signing the registers of Juvenile Employment Bureaux of Local Education Authorities.

IX

RELATIVE NUMBERS OF MEN AND WOMEN IN INDUSTRY

THE view is widely held that the number of women in industry has greatly increased relatively to men during recent years. It is true that the proportion of women in certain occupations is considerably greater than before the war or in early post-war years, and these increases are no doubt responsible for the view that there has been a large general growth in the numbers of women in industry. Statistics show, however, that the increase in the proportion of women has only been slight, and in no sense constitutes a serious general problem. This is equally true in West Yorkshire as in Great Britain as a whole. One example of an appreciable increase in Great Britain in the proportion of women between the 1921 and 1931 Censuses is in general engineering;[1] mention may also be made of the increase in the proportion of women in the manufacture of leather goods (bags, trunks, etc.), and in furniture making. On the other hand, the proportion of men to women has decreased in agriculture, building and brick making, printing (newspapers and books), artificial silk, tobacco, many branches of commerce and finance and in Government services, both central

[1] This has been due more to decline in the number of men than to increase in the number of women.

and local. Two opposite tendencies are, indeed, operating; more opportunities in industry, commerce, and the professions are available for women, but a rising standard of living diminishes the incentive to use these opportunities.

The following figures show the general change throughout West Yorkshire industry according to the 1921 and 1931 Census returns, in comparison with the change in Great Britain. These Census figures are calculated from data for the whole of the West Riding by deducting the numbers in Barnsley, Doncaster, Rotherham, Sheffield, and York. The area is, therefore, considerably larger than West Yorkshire as defined at the beginning of this review; it includes a number of residential towns, for example Harrogate and Ilkley, and also agricultural areas, in which the proportion of women employed is considerably less than in the chief West Yorkshire towns, particularly those in which the textile industry is important.

PERSONS IN INDUSTRY IN WEST YORKSHIRE*

		Males	*Females*
1921	..	.. 815,001	355,284
1931	..	.. 894,569	397,137

NUMBER OF FEMALES TO EACH 100 MALES

		West Yorkshire	*Great Britain*†
1921	..	.. 43·6	41·7
1931	..	.. 44·4	42·4

* Including persons unemployed. The 1921 figures include children from 12 years of age, whereas the 1931 figures include only children from 14 years of age.

† The corresponding number at the time of the 1911 Census was 42·2.

These statistics show small increases in the proportion of females to males in industry both in West Yorkshire and in the country as a whole, the rate of increase being almost identical. They also show a higher proportion of females to males in West Yorkshire industries than in Great Britain, this being largely due to the great employment of women and girls in the woollen and worsted industry and in clothing manufacture.

As already indicated, the proportion of women employed in the textile towns of West Yorkshire is considerably higher than in the area covered by the Census figures given above. This is shown by the statistics tabulated on page 101 of insured men and women in the twelve chief towns in July 1924 and July 1935. The statistics reflect a slight increase during the period covered in the proportion of women in the twelve towns together, from 53·3 to 54·9 per cent. The greatest number of women to each hundred men was in Bradford. Castleford is in marked contrast with the other towns, having easily the lowest percentage; the increase in the percentage between 1924 and 1935 is due more to a diminution in the number of men than to an increase in the number of women. The low percentages in Castleford are due to the predominance of coal-mining, but considerable numbers of women residing in Castleford are employed in other centres. Similarly, numbers of people residing in other towns are employed outside their town of residence.

ESTIMATED NUMBERS OF INSURED MEN AND WOMEN AGED 18 TO 64 IN TWELVE WEST YORKSHIRE TOWNS, AT JULY 1924 AND JULY 1935, AND COMPARISON WITH GREAT BRITAIN AND NORTHERN IRELAND

Town	JULY 1924			JULY 1935		
	Men	Women	Number of women per 100 men	Men	Women	Number of women per 100 men
Batley	8,620	5,500	63·8	7,330	4,720	64·4
Bradford	63,720	45,060	68·9	66,010	44,500	67·4
Castleford	22,300	830	3·7	19,150	1,190	6·2
Dewsbury	11,690	7,060	60·4	12,610	6,510	51·6
Halifax	21,980	13,740	62·5	23,640	14,070	59·5
Huddersfield	31,490	16,370	52·0	33,210	16,040	48·3
Keighley	11,590	5,760	49·7	10,380	6,240	60·1
Leeds	88,710	52,090	58·7	106,460	66,390	62·4
Morley	9,180	5,280	57·5	7,750	4,960	64·0
Shipley	8,160	5,370	65·8	7,860	4,770	60·7
Spenborough	11,210	4,280	38·2	10,530	5,090	48·3
Wakefield	22,270	4,480	20·1	22,740	5,530	24·3
Totals, West Yorkshire towns	310,920	165,820	53·3	327,670	180,010	54·9
Totals, Great Britain and Northern Ireland*	8,476,800	3,031,200	35·8	9,531,000	3,527,000	37·0

* The figures for Great Britain and Northern Ireland include juveniles 16 to 18 years of age; the 1924 figures also include a number of insured persons over 64 years of age.

Certain statistical considerations also render detailed comparisons between the different centres somewhat unsatisfactory.

The position in some of the chief industries is shown by the table opposite. Coal mining, building, and road transportation are omitted as the proportion of insured women employed in these industries is very small. The statistics show only slight changes between 1924 and 1935 in the proportions of women, but they show very wide variations from industry to industry. Tailoring has easily the highest proportion of women, with more than five women to two men. Wool and worsted has a proportion of about three women to two men, while in printing and bookbinding and the distributive trades there is approximately one insured woman to two men. Textile dyeing and finishing is largely a man's trade, with only about one insured woman to five men. It is of special interest to note the low percentage of women in general engineering. The increase in the percentage from 4·5 in 1924 to 5·9 in 1935 is due more to decline in the number of men than to increase in the number of women. It is evident that there has been no considerable increase in the number of women in general engineering in West Yorkshire, and that in this area it remains predominantly a men's industry.

This section may be concluded by comparing the rates of unemployment among men and women. According to the unemployment insurance statistics

ESTIMATED NUMBERS OF INSURED MEN AND WOMEN AGED 18 TO 64 IN VARIOUS INDUSTRIES IN WEST YORKSHIRE JULY 1924 AND JULY 1935

	JULY 1924			JULY 1935		
Industry	*Men*	*Women*	*Percentage of women to men*	*Men*	*Women*	*Percentage of women to men*
Woollen and worsted	58,560	88,200	150·6	53,570	79,020	147·5
Textile dyeing, etc.	11,330	2,750	24·3	8,590	1,880	21·9
Tailoring	8,550	22,410	262·1	11,820	31,630	267·6
General engineering	38,640	1,750	4·5	32,850	1,950	5·9
Printing and bookbinding ..	5,540	2,850	51·5	7,130	3,840	53·8
Distributive trades	27,650	14,350	51·8	40,080	20,610	51·4

men suffer from a much higher rate of unemployment than women. This is due to a variety of causes, including the influence of the lower rates of wages paid to women, and the greater tendency for women to withdraw from industry if their employment becomes irregular.

The following figures give a comparison of the percentages of unemployment among men and women. They are for the twelve largest towns of West Yorkshire, and show the percentages for all industries at May 1935 and also for six important industries, mainly those in which considerable numbers of women are employed.

UNEMPLOYMENT PERCENTAGES
MAY 1935

Industry	*Men*	*Women*
Wool and worsted	17·1	11·4
Textile dyeing and finishing	25·7	10·0
Tailoring	6·5	2·2
Printing and bookbinding	11·1	9·0
General engineering*	11·1	5·7
Distributive trades	11·8	4·8
All industries†	17·9	9·1

* As already indicated, the number of women employed in this industry in West Yorkshire is small, but it is included here because of the considerable interest shown in female labour in engineering.

† This group includes a large number of other industries in addition to the six given above.

The figures show that the rate of unemployment among men is almost double that among women.

The smallest difference in the industries given is in printing and bookbinding. In tailoring, which shows the lowest unemployment percentages for both men and women, the women's rate is only one-third of the men's rate. The figure of 2·2 per cent for women in this industry is so low as to represent a distinct shortage of female labour during periods of good seasonal activity. In the distributive trades also the percentage is low.

X

JUVENILE EMPLOYMENT AND UNEMPLOYMENT

THE demand for juvenile labour, especially between fourteen and sixteen years of age, has been maintained at a high level during post-war years in most of the chief centres of West Yorkshire. In consequence, unemployment has remained almost negligible except during two or three years of the depression. Even in those years juvenile unemployment was relatively slight, this being due largely to the fact that the depression coincided with a sharp decline in the numbers leaving school owing to the low birth-rate of the war period. Since the depression there has been a shortage of juvenile workers in the textile and clothing centres. The reports of Juvenile Employment Sub-Committees indicate that, in these centres, girls are absorbed into industry more quickly than boys. The shortage is made good by bringing in mainly girls from the predominantly mining centres of West Yorkshire (Castleford and Pontefract) where there is an insufficiency of suitable openings, and also, to a small extent, from depressed areas in other parts of the country.

The Census returns provide a basis for studying the potential supply of juvenile labour. According to the 1931 Census the total number of juveniles aged 14 to 17 years in the twelve largest towns of West Yorkshire was 79,880. Of these 38,436 were boys and 41,444 were girls. A considerable number were continuing their education or for other reasons were not in employment or seeking employment. They were distributed between the different towns as follows:

			Boys	*Girls*	*Total*
Batley ..	..	..	1,044	1,136	2,180
Bradford	..	..	8,191	8,997	17,188
Castleford	..	..	830	781	1,611
Dewsbury	..	..	1,849	1,867	3,716
Halifax	..	..	2,761	2,999	5,760
Huddersfield	..	..	3,160	3,431	6,591
Keighley	..	..	1,145	1,150	2,295
Leeds ..	..	..	15,156	16,489	31,645
Morley ..	..	..	761	776	1,537
Spenborough ..	..	..	910	992	1,902
Shipley	..	..	854	970	1,824
Wakefield	..	..	1,775	1,856	3,631

The numbers shown by the 1931 Census were, however, abnormally low owing to the smaller number of children born during the war. The total numbers in normal years would be at least 12 per cent higher.[1] Account must, however, be taken of the effect of the declining birth-rate, which will result in a reduction after about 1937 in the number of juveniles leaving school, while the shortage of juvenile labour will be accentuated by the raising

[1] The 1921 Census showed a total of 93,000 juveniles, 14 to 17 years of age, in the twelve towns compared with 79,880 in 1931.

of the school-leaving age. These changes will involve certain adjustments in undertakings which have hitherto employed large numbers of juveniles.

From September 3, 1934, the unemployment insurance system was extended to cover juveniles leaving school at the earliest age, and statistics then became available showing the numbers of juveniles aged 14 to 17 years in insured trades. The following table shows the estimated numbers of insured boys and girls between these ages in twelve West Yorkshire towns at July 1935:

	Boys	Girls	Total
Batley	680	710	1,390
Bradford	6,400	6,800	13,200
Castleford	2,030	590	2,620
Dewsbury	1,330	1,200	2,530
Halifax	2,220	2,510	4,730
Huddersfield	2,800	2,700	5,570
Keighley	1,020	1,040	2,060
Leeds	13,460	14,590	28,050
Morley	730	710	1,440
Spenborough	1,160	1,350	2,510
Shipley	720	880	1,600
Wakefield	2,130	1,880	4,010
Totals	34,680	35,030	69,710

These statistics do not include children continuing their education at day school, or remaining at home without desiring paid work, or employed in occupations not covered by the unemployment insurance system, e.g. domestic service. They are affected by the abnormal birth-rates during and immediately after the war, there being, however, compensation between the low birth-rate in 1918 and the high birth-rate in 1920. The total of about 70,000 insured boys and girls in the twelve towns is divided almost equally between the two sexes.

The estimated numbers of insured boys and girls in each of the chief industries at July 1935 are given below. The woollen and worsted industry is the largest field of employment of juvenile labour, and is followed by the distributive trades and tailoring, each of which employs more than 10,000 boys and girls. In the woollen and worsted and tailoring industries girls predominate, while in the distributive trades the number of boys is considerably greater than that of girls. General engineering provides employment for over 4,000 boys and youths under 18 years of age.

ESTIMATED NUMBERS OF INSURED JUVENILES AT JULY 1935 IN THE CHIEF WEST YORKSHIRE TOWNS, BY INDUSTRIES

Industry	Boys	Girls	Total
Wool and worsted ..	6,490	11,000	17,490
Distributive trades ..	6,220	4,650	10,870
Tailoring	2,480	7,910	10,390
General engineering ..	4,020	490	4,510
Coal-mining	2,220	—	2,220
Printing	890	1,220	2,110
Building	1,870	—	1,870
Textile dyeing ..	710	390	1,100
Road transport ..	450	20	470
Other industries ..	9,330	9,350	18,680
Totals	34,680	35,030	69,710

Statistics of the number of unemployed juveniles on the registers in twelve West Yorkshire towns are tabulated on page 111 for May and November during recent years. The data are not strictly comparable owing to the effects of administrative changes and especially to the extension from September 1934 of compulsory insurance to boys and girls aged 14 and 15 years. This latter factor, by ensuring more complete registration, partly explains the greater numbers shown for November 1934 and May 1935 compared with the two previous periods, but the numbers at this time were also affected by the high birth-rate in the years immediately after the war. The figures for dates before September 1934 are appreciably below the actual numbers owing to failure of some boys and girls aged 14 and 15 to register before compulsory unemployment insurance applied to them.

During the depression the rate of unemployment among juveniles probably averaged around 6 to 8 per cent. Before the depression began and in 1935 and 1936 the rate was about 2 per cent or even less, this representing a shortage of labour. Usually the rates have been appreciably lower for girls than boys. The highest figure shown in the table was in November 1930, when the number on the unemployment registers was approximately 4,000, and, as has already been indicated, this number is probably somewhat too low. By the end of 1935 the total had fallen to about 1,000. May and June are usually

NUMBER OF UNEMPLOYED JUVENILES AGED 14 TO 17 YEARS ON THE REGISTERS IN TWELVE WEST YORKSHIRE TOWNS AT MAY AND NOVEMBER 1924, AND 1928 TO 1936

Date			Boys	Girls	Total
1924					
May ..	..	..	226	193	419
November	..	..	430	561	991
1928					
May ..	..	..	619	535	1,154
November	..	..	1,183	1,238	2,421
1929					
May ..	..	..	903	655	1,558
November	..	..	1,361	1,002	2,363
1930					
May ..	..	..	1,618	1,608	3,226
November	..	..	2,227	1,728	3,955
1931					
May ..	..	..	1,882	1,587	3,469
November	..	..	1,769	1,065	2,834
1932					
May ..	..	..	1,265	1,117	2,382
November	..	..	1,498	1,139	2,637
1933					
May ..	..	..	1,089	591	1,680
November	..	..	691	411	1,102
1934					
May ..	..	..	589	416	1,005
November	..	..	996	610	1,600
1935					
May ..	..	..	934	616	1,550
November	..	..	630	433	1,063
1936					
May*	..	..	455	347	802

* Provisional.

the best months for juvenile employment, while the numbers unemployed are highest at the end of each school term, especially in July and August, when the numbers are temporarily swollen by school-leavers who have not yet found employment. During the depression, Junior Instruction Centres for unemployed juveniles were opened in a number of towns, but with the progress of industrial recovery resulting in a substantial fall in the numbers out of work, and in a shortening of the period of unemployment of individuals, the centres became difficult to organize and were subsequently closed.

The problem of juvenile labour in West Yorkshire is not unemployment but the risk of entering blind-alley occupations. Juveniles tend to take jobs where wages at the outset are relatively high even though the ultimate prospects are poor. An increase is required in training facilities for adult employment.

XI

CONCLUSIONS

WEST YORKSHIRE is a compact industrial area with a population of about 1,500,000 and about 670,000 insured workpeople. In its industrial structure, which shows considerable unity, the woollen and worsted industry gives the area its character. The number of insured workpeople in this industry is about 140,000, while to these must be added the numbers in the directly associated industries of textile dyeing and finishing, and tailoring. The industry also consumes a considerable amount of coal and electrical power produced in the area. Much engineering work is engaged in the production of textile machinery and power plant for the mills, and many services, particularly in the distributive trades and road transportation, together with building, are developed largely to supply the needs of workers in the woollen and worsted and associated industries.

To a considerable extent, therefore, West Yorkshire is dependent upon the prosperity of one group of associated industries. This dependence is, however, somewhat smaller than in some other parts of the country. A wide variety of industries is established in the area, and this is one of the reasons why West Yorkshire has weathered the storm of the great depression more easily than several other areas.

H

Another factor has been the greater extent to which its products are sold in the home market, so that a large part of its industry has been less affected by the collapse of foreign trade than in the great exporting districts.

During the depression West Yorkshire suffered more severely from unemployment than the country as a whole, but this has been compensated by a more rapid recovery. According to the experience of the last twelve years, West Yorkshire enjoys a better record than the country as a whole in good times, but is liable to deeper depression. The area provided employment for a greater number of workpeople in the summer of 1936 than in earlier periods, and, in view of improvements in the efficiency of industry, the volume of production in West Yorkshire must now be greater than ever before. The rate of unemployment, however, remained somewhat higher than before the depression. In May 1932— the worst year of the depression—the number of adult insured workers unemployed in the twelve chief towns of West Yorkshire exceeded 113,000; four years later the numbers had fallen to less than one-half.

Though its record has been more favourable than that of the "special" or depressed areas of the country, West Yorkshire has a supply of labour surplus to her present industrial needs. This surplus may be estimated at about 18,000 to 20,000 workpeople, mainly men. This number is much smaller than those estimated for the severely depressed areas where industrial surveys were initiated by the Government a few years ago. In the course of these surveys the following estimates were made of the surplus labour supply of the various districts:

Lancashire, with Merseyside	186,000
South-West Scotland	100,000
North-East Coast	64,000
South Wales	50,000

For these districts transference of a considerable part of their surplus labour to other areas is essential for a solution of their difficulties. West Yorkshire is faced with a much smaller problem. Given maintenance of reasonably good trade conditions, West Yorkshire should experience little difficulty during the next ten or twelve years in absorbing into industry the relatively small number of workpeople who are, under present conditions, surplus to her needs. This would not mean the elimination of unemployment; in every district there is always a number of workpeople unemployed temporarily for various reasons, including seasonal factors, while the course of trade suffers from fluctuations of the trade cycle, and, during cyclical depressions, workpeople who are not surplus to the needs of their district suffer from unemployment. Under good cyclical conditions of trade West Yorkshire has a "minimum" volume of unemployment of over 40,000 workpeople, a large part of whom represent a "normal" reserve of labour. This is additional to the surplus mentioned in the preceding paragraph.

The whole of the post-war period has been one of rapid technical, economic, and social change, and the industrial structure of West Yorkshire has undergone considerable modification. This has tended to increase the numbers unemployed. It has also resulted in expansion of some branches of industry and decline of others. The general tendency has been for the numbers employed in manufacturing industries to decline during the period from 1924 to 1936, and for various services to expand. A tendency has been operating for labour released by mechanization from the manufacturing industries to be employed in personal services. The highest rates of expansion are shown by certain branches of the electrical industry, while high rates are also shown for brick and tile making (as a result of the building boom), road transportation services, construction and repair of motor vehicles, cycles, and aircraft, artificial silk, and laundry and dry-cleaning services. Then come the distributive trades, professional services, entertainments and sports, hotel, restaurant, and boarding-house service; tailoring, building, and printing also stand high. The greatest increases in numbers, as distinct from the highest rates of expansion, have taken place in the distributive trades, tailoring, road transportation, and building.

The outstanding declines have been in the woollen and worsted industry, textile dyeing and finishing, coal-mining, and general engineering. Mention may also be made of the declines in railway carriage and wagon making, and in various branches of the leather industry. With the recovery of trade, especially in 1935 and 1936, the shrinkage of some of the declining industries seems to have come to an end. A study of the expanding and declining industries shows the need for the continuous opening up of new fields of employment if the prosperity of the area is to be maintained.

There has been a slight increase during the last twelve years in the proportion of females to males in West Yorkshire industry. The proportion of females to males in industry is high in West Yorkshire compared with the country as a whole, this being largely due to the large numbers of women and girls employed in the woollen and worsted and clothing industries. The rate of unemployment among women is much lower than that among men, being little more than one-half. Among unemployed men in the twelve chief West Yorkshire towns about 42 per cent in November 1935 were over forty-five years of age, this being a distinctly higher percentage than in the country as a whole. As regards duration of unemployment, more than 20,000 persons at November 1935 had been unemployed for three months or more, and no less than 2,818 of these had been out of work continuously for three years or more. Juvenile unemployment is negligible except during years of depression; in times of good trade there is shortage of juveniles, and arrangements are

made to attract boys and girls to the chief manufacturing centres from outlying districts.

It is outside the scope of this statistical review to
examine in detail technical, economic, and social
factors which have been responsible for the various
changes and trends. Reference has already been made
to the loss of foreign trade, and the consequent
tendency to adapt industry more to the needs of
the home market. This process has been facilitated
by tariffs, especially in certain branches of the
woollen and worsted industry and engineering.
However, some expansion of the export trade may
be looked for. The worst period of trade restrictions
throughout the world seems to be over, while the
threatened shortage of gold so much discussed during
the period from 1927 to 1930 as a deflationary and
depressing factor has disappeared for the present
as a result of currency devaluations and stimulus to
gold production. West Yorkshire industry has benefited, along with industry throughout the country,
from expanded purchasing power, the building
boom, rearmament, cheap money, and freedom
from the over-valuation of sterling which was a
handicap during the first decade after the war.
These various factors have contributed to the recent
recovery, and, apart from the danger of international
conflict, they make the industrial outlook reasonably
favourable.

APPENDIX I

NOTES ON THE STATISTICS USED IN THIS REVIEW

(1) The statistics upon which this review is based are those compiled by the Ministry of Labour in the administration of the Unemployment Insurance Acts. Comparability over a period of years is affected by legislative and administrative changes in the conditions for the receipt of unemployment benefit, but the statistics are sufficiently comparable to enable general trends to be reviewed.

(2) The figures for any town relate to the employment exchange or exchanges in the town, and do not purport to represent the numbers of *residents* in the town in the different industrial categories. The estimated numbers of insured persons in the area of any employment exchange are based on the numbers of unemployment books which were exchanged there at the time of the annual exchange of such books. Books may be exchanged singly by insured persons themselves, or in bulk by employers on behalf of all their employees; and when the latter course is adopted it may frequently happen that an insured worker's book is exchanged at an employment exchange other than the one at which he would register when unemployed, since the exchange which is nearest to his place of work is not necessarily the nearest to his place of residence.

(3) The Ministry of Labour's statistics for the years before 1928 include persons aged sixteen years and over, while those from 1928 onwards cover only persons aged sixteen to sixty-four. To ensure greater comparability the statistics given in this review for the years earlier

than 1928 have been reduced by proportions representing as far as possible the numbers of persons over sixty-four years of age. For this purpose proportions for the whole country obtained by a sample inquiry in 1926 conducted by the Ministry of Labour have been used. It must be noted that the proportions in West Yorkshire would not be the same as those in the country as a whole, though the differences are probably not great. Also the assumption is made that the proportions in 1926 are applicable to earlier years (1923 and 1924).

(4) The statistics of the numbers of persons in employment have been calculated by deducting the numbers unemployed from the estimated numbers of insured persons. No allowance has, however, been made for the numbers directly involved in trade disputes, or for absences from work through sickness or other forms of unrecorded non-employment other than "recognized" holidays. For the latter causes (sickness, etc.) the Ministry of Labour makes, for the whole country, an allowance of $3\frac{1}{2}$ per cent of the numbers insured.

(5) The statistics given for Leeds are totals for the Leeds, Armley, and Stanningley employment exchanges.

APPENDIX II

STATISTICS OF ESTIMATED NUMBERS OF INSURED PERSONS, NUMBERS AND PERCENTAGES UNEMPLOYED IN CERTAIN INDUSTRIES IN GREAT BRITAIN AND NORTHERN IRELAND, 1924 AND 1928 TO 1936

STATISTICS for Great Britain and Northern Ireland are tabulated below for each of the nine industries for which statistics for West Yorkshire were reviewed in Section VI. The statistics tabulated for West Yorkshire cover only adult workpeople, whereas those for Great Britain and Northern Ireland include also juveniles 16 to 18 years of age. They are, however, useful for the purpose of comparing general trends in West Yorkshire with those in the country as a whole.

In addition to the tables for Great Britain and Northern Ireland, which have been compiled from the Ministry of Labour Gazette, two tables taken from *The Economist*, July 11, 1936, are given in which comparisons are made of employment, numbers insured, and percentages unemployed in 1929, 1932, and 1935 in each of fourteen large towns in different parts of the country, including the two largest towns of West Yorkshire—Leeds and Bradford. These tables are compiled from the Ministry of Labour's statistics, and are subject to the qualifications given in Appendix I.

WOOLLEN AND WORSTED INDUSTRY, MALES AND FEMALES

Year	Estimated numbers insured*	NUMBERS UNEMPLOYED		PERCENTAGE UNEMPLOYED	
		May	November	May	November
1924	251,070	12,388	21,794	4·9	8·7
1928	242,590	20,901	33,966	8·6	14·0
1929	239,030	27,917	35,802	11·7	15·0
1930	240,460	53,395	60,320	22·2	25·1
1931	238,870	64,833	42,819	27·1	17·9
1932	233,610	60,872	40,972	26·1	17·5
1933	230,880	32,733	21,274	14·2	9·2
1934	229,590	36,501	30,353	15·9	13·2
1935	221,720	33,193	18,075	14·9	8·2
1936	—	21,936	—	9·9†	—

* Figures for July.

† This percentage for May is the relation between the number unemployed in May 1936 and the estimated number of insured persons at July 1935. For previous years the percentages both for May and November are calculated by using the estimated number insured at July of the same year.

TEXTILE DYEING AND FINISHING, MALES AND FEMALES

Year	Estimated numbers insured*	NUMBERS UNEMPLOYED		PERCENTAGE UNEMPLOYED	
		May	*November*	*May*	*November*
1924	112,060	14,054	13,841	12·5	12·4
1928	116,670	12,171	18,478	10·4	15·8
1929	116,230	20,390	20,568	17·5	17·7
1930	116,900	35,348	43,433	30·2	37·2
1931	115,000	38,382	36,696	33·4	31·9
1932	112,090	32,706	31,596	29·2	28·2
1933	113,140	27,377	24,233	24·2	21·4
1934	109,530	24,516	23,656	22·6	21·6
1935	108,510	24,515	23,105	22·6	21·3
1936	—	19,627	—	18·1†	—

* Figures for July.   † Footnote as for Woollen and Worsted Industry.

TAILORING, MALES AND FEMALES

Year	Estimated numbers insured*	NUMBERS UNEMPLOYED		PERCENTAGE UNEMPLOYED	
		May	November	May	November
1924	186,610	8,460	24,686	4·5	13·2
1928	198,880	4,548	25,293	2·3	12·7
1929	199,350	7,153	21,518	3·6	10·8
1930	201,830	11,812	34,605	5·9	17·1
1931	213,020	18,021	39,722	8·5	18·6
1932	211,660	22,598	43,425	10·7	20·5
1933	216,660	24,540	33,143	11·8	15·3
1934	208,900	14,671	33,677	7·0	16·1
1935	208,750	14,553	31,609	7·0	15·1
1936	—	13,141	—	6·3†	—

* Figures for July. † Footnote as for Woollen and Worsted Industry.

GENERAL ENGINEERING, MALES

Year	Estimated numbers insured*	NUMBERS UNEMPLOYED		PERCENTAGE UNEMPLOYED	
		May	*November*	*May*	*November*
1924	566,430	98,276	89,596	17·4	15·3
1928	536,550	53,801	59,006	10·0	11·0
1929	539,330	53,640	57,980	9·9	10·8
1930	542,540	82,738	126,578	15·3	23·3
1931	528,910	153,447	152,997	29·0	28·9
1932	507,690	159,762	160,600	31·5	31·6
1933	486,520	127,983	108,204	26·3	21·0
1934	478,570	83,136	71,347	17·4	14·9
1935	484,750	66,700	56,876	13·8	11·7
1936	—	45,123	—	9·3†	—

* Figures for July. † Footnote as for Woollen and Worsted Industry.

COAL-MINING, MALES

Year	Estimated numbers insured*	NUMBERS UNEMPLOYED		PERCENTAGE UNEMPLOYED	
		May	November	May	November
1924	1,215,860	36,980	109,414	3·0	9·0
1928	1,109,800	244,730	281,286	22·1	25·3
1929	1,069,180	199,223	152,867	18·6	14·3
1930	1,063,350	235,472	224,512	22·1	21·1
1931	1,041,120	287,899	282,659	27·6	27·1
1932	1,039,840	337,033	355,338	32·4	34·2
1933	1,019,140	383,449	310,287	37·6	30·4
1934	977,160	292,436	250,196	29·9	25·6
1935	934,420	262,215	189,450	28·6	20·3
1936	—	215,998	—	23·1†	—

* Figures for July.

† Footnote as for Woollen and Worsted Industry.

PRINTING AND BOOKBINDING, MALES AND FEMALES

Year	Estimated numbers insured*	NUMBERS UNEMPLOYED		PERCENTAGE UNEMPLOYED	
		May	November	May	November
1924	234,230	11,967	12,222	5·1	5·2
1928	253,640	10,826	10,776	4·3	4·2
1929	261,130	10,046	12,004	3·8	4·6
1930	272,390	16,742	22,356	6·1	8·2
1931	278,970	27,476	30,859	9·8	11·1
1932	284,770	30,456	29,032	10·7	10·2
1933	284,950	26,918	25,827	9·5	9·1
1934	279,730	24,647	23,651	8·8	8·5
1935	277,420	23,182	22,604	8·4	8·1
1936	—	21,849	—	7·9†	—

* Figures for July.   † Footnote as for Woollen and Worsted Industry.

BUILDING, MALES

Year	Estimated numbers insured*	NUMBERS UNEMPLOYED		PERCENTAGE UNEMPLOYED	
		May	*November*	*May*	*November*
1924	679,230	56,467	77,487	8·3	11·4
1928	807,650	74,917	120,289	9·3	14·9
1929	816,780	72,196	132,159	8·8	16·2
1930	822,770	104,127	174,301	12·7	21·2
1931	848,250	150,315	231,093	17·7	27·2
1932	846,830	226,162	264,757	26·7	31·3
1933	873,540	175,132	187,439	20·0	21·5
1934	917,330	137,089	183,257	14·9	20·0
1935	965,810	135,234	164,601	14·3	17·0
1936	—	107,658	—	11·1†	—

* Figures for July.   † Footnote as for Woollen and Worsted Industry.

DISTRIBUTIVE TRADES, MALES AND FEMALES

Year	*Estimated numbers insured**	NUMBERS UNEMPLOYED		PERCENTAGE UNEMPLOYED	
		May	*November*	*May*	*November*
1924	1,327,900	80,060	91,931	6·0	6·9
1928	1,613,790	82,281	100,894	5·1	6·3
1929	1,679,090	95,311	112,302	5·7	6·7
1930	1,764,390	146,065	185,946	8·3	10·5
1931	1,874,780	206,816	240,173	11·0	12·8
1932	1,950,240	231,366	247,261	11·9	12·7
1933	1,992,000	225,051	229,598	11·3	11·5
1934	2,005,340	215,685	225,165	10·8	11·2
1935	2,007,340	221,815	219,605	11·1	10·9
1936	—	202,710	—	10·1†	—

* Figures for July. † Footnote as for Woollen and Worsted Industry.

I

ROAD TRANSPORTATION, MALES

Year	Estimated numbers insured*	NUMBERS UNEMPLOYED		PERCENTAGE UNEMPLOYED	
		May	*November*	*May*	*November*
1924	254,530	24,893	26,345	9·8	10·4
1928	304,870	21,630	27,315	7·1	9·0
1929	337,310	24,123	28,843	7·2	8·6
1930	336,980	33,581	42,488	10·0	12·6
1931	362,330	43,825	53,805	12·1	14·8
1932	373,370	53,969	61,349	14·5	16·4
1933	375,780	52,637	56,255	14·0	15·0
1934	379,020	49,964	51,280	13·2	13·5
1935	386,660	48,056	46,236	12·4	12·0
1936	—	39,804	—	10·3†	—

* Figures for July.   † Footnote as for Woollen and Worsted Industry.

ALL INDUSTRIES, MALES AND FEMALES

Year	Estimated numbers insured*	NUMBERS UNEMPLOYED		PERCENTAGE UNEMPLOYED	
		May	November	May	November
1924	11,330,300	1,059,660	1,237,330	9·4	10·9
1928	11,881,500	1,168,009	1,453,217	9·8	12·1
1929	12,094,000	1,177,484	1,325,605	9·7	10·9
1930	12,405,700	1,855,898	2,368,798	15·0	19·1
1931	12,770,000	2,577,916	2,734,854	20·2	21·4
1932	12,808,000	2,821,840	2,849,025	22·0	22·2
1933	12,883,000	2,496,053	2,308,779	19·4	17·9
1934	12,960,000	2,097,251	2,122,299	16·2	16·4
1935	13,058,000	2,024,463	1,905,675	15·5	14·6
1936	—	1,696,920	—	13·0†	—

* Figures for July.   † Footnote as for Woollen and Worsted Industry.

INDEX OF NUMBERS EMPLOYED IN VARIOUS TOWNS IN GREAT BRITAIN
IN 1932 AND 1935*

(1929 = 100)

	1932	1935
London Division	98	108
Birmingham	93	112
Bristol	92	99
Nottingham (including Netherfield) ..	100	106
Stoke	85	100
Bradford	93	103
Hull	99	102
Leeds	93	106
Newcastle-on-Tyne	92	100
Sheffield	77	94
Liverpool and Bootle	91	94
Manchester	93	98
Edinburgh	99	102
Glasgow	86	93

* Statistics published in *The Economist*, July 11, 1936. The figures are for July of each year.

ESTIMATED NUMBERS INSURED AND PERCENTAGE UNEMPLOYED IN VARIOUS TOWNS IN GREAT BRITAIN IN 1929, 1932, AND 1935*

	ESTIMATED NUMBERS INSURED			PERCENTAGE UNEMPLOYED		
	1929	*1932*	*1935*	*1929*	*1932*	*1935*
London Division..	2,214,430	2,366,200	2,466,310	4·4	12·6	7·5
Birmingham	365,620	381,850	410,330	6·1	16·1	6·5
Bristol	130,980	133,880	133,870	10·3	19·7	13·4
Nottingham (including Nether-field)	108,750	116,530	119,800	9·4	15·5	12·8
Stoke	113,680	119,070	120,690	16·3	32·0	21·1
Bradford	118,260	119,200	116,660	15·7	22·3	12·0
Hull	87,560	94,080	92,820	13·2	19·6	16·5
Leeds	167,630	179,390	184,460	9·5	21·6	12·5
Newcastle-on-Tyne	108,350	117,010	118,920	15·0	27·8	22·9
Sheffield	167,030	170,570	170,280	13·7	35·1	20·3
Liverpool and Bootle	313,730	334,070	334,690	16·0	28·0	26·1
Manchester	348,980	359,970	363,870	7·0	16·1	12·7
Edinburgh	123,200	131,610	134,750	9·8	16·3	16·0
Glasgow	376,320	402,500	406,910	12·8	30·2	25·0

* Statistics published in *The Economist*, July 11, 1936. The data are for July of each year. The percentages unemployed express the relation between the numbers unemployed and the estimated numbers insured. The estimated numbers insured cover persons aged 16 to 64 years in all industries.

APPENDIX III

STATISTICS SHOWING THE ESTIMATED NUMBERS OF INSURED PERSONS IN THE CHIEF INDUSTRIES OF WEST YORK-SHIRE AT JULY 1935, BY TOWNS

STATISTICS are tabulated below showing the estimated numbers of insured persons aged 16 to 64 years in forty-three of the most important industries in West Yorkshire, by towns, at July 1935. They give an indication in some detail of the industrial structure of West Yorkshire. They are subject to the qualifications mentioned in Note 2 of Appendix I.

Town	Coal mining	Stone quarrying and mining	Brick, tile, etc., making	Glass trades	Chemicals, etc.
Batley ..	360	—	30	—	160
Bradford ..	330	290	140	80	460
Castleford ..	15,130	10	170	900	150
Dewsbury ..	1,540	—	20	—	180
Halifax ..	160	610	1,070	10	180
Huddersfield ..	480	250	210	10	3,220
Keighley ..	10	20	40	—	110
Leeds	2,150	200	1,790	790	2,710
Morley ..	630	200	60	340	50
Shipley ..	20	30	70	—	20
Spenborough	520	—	—	40	370
Wakefield ..	7,310	—	150	180	160

Town	Iron and steel rolling, forging, etc.	Wire, wire netting, wire ropes	General engineering, etc.	Electrical engineering	Motor vehicles, etc.
Batley ..	—	—	420	30	80
Bradford ..	200	210	4,380	1,830	1,210
Castleford ..	—	—	40	—	10
Dewsbury ..	30	—	170	60	50
Halifax ..	—	640	3,630	40	180
Huddersfield ..	—	—	5,300	330	760
Keighley ..	—	—	4,210	10	110
Leeds	780	10	12,840	470	1,840
Morley ..	—	50	740	10	20
Shipley ..	10	—	1,090	10	140
Spenborough	—	1,190	1,780	—	170
Wakefield ..	—	540	2,220	10	120

Town	Railway carriages, wagons, etc.	General iron founding, etc.	Electrical wiring and contracting	Brass and allied metal wares	Woollen and worsted
Batley ..	—	—	10	—	7,760
Bradford ..	40	310	340	200	47,310
Castleford ..	—	30	10	10	50
Dewsbury ..	60	30	20	—	9,070
Halifax ..	—	140	130	770	11,840
Huddersfield ..	30	110	100	10	18,900
Keighley ..	10	280	70	—	6,570
Leeds	100	2,890	480	840	15,150
Morley ..	—	—	10	160	7,430
Shipley ..	—	40	10	—	6,920
Spenborough	—	20	10	—	4,600
Wakefield ..	1,090	—	70	—	4,770

Town	Artificial silk (weaving, etc.)	Carpets	Textile dyeing, etc.	Tanning, currying, and dressing	Tailoring
Batley ..	—	190	480	—	320
Bradford ..	4,020	10	5,440	50	810
Castleford ..	—	—	—	—	140
Dewsbury ..	60	230	180	140	30
Halifax ..	430	1,940	680	20	150
Huddersfield ..	50	220	1,580	—	1,550
Keighley ..	300	—	540	70	50
Leeds	—	140	1,090	2,050	44,560
Morley ..	40	10	110	440	50
Shipley ..	100	—	500	50	20
Spenborough	50	2,570	480	310	20
Wakefield ..	—	120	10	40	110

Town	Dress-making and millinery	Shirts, under-clothing, etc.	Boots, shoes, etc.	Bread, cakes, etc.	Cocoa, chocolate, etc.
Batley ..	10	10	10	180	—
Bradford ..	890	540	170	1,630	20
Castleford ..	10	—	20	20	220
Dewsbury ..	10	140	—	110	10
Halifax ..	80	1,010	60	500	1,100
Huddersfield ..	50	90	90	360	30
Keighley ..	110	20	20	90	40
Leeds	650	1,350	2,570	1,490	690
Morley ..	—	—	10	50	20
Shipley ..	—	190	30	100	—
Spenborough	10	200	340	90	100
Wakefield ..	20	300	60	90	60

Town		Drink industries	Furniture, woodwork, etc.	Cardboard boxes, stationery, etc.	Printing, bookbinding, etc.	Building
Batley	..	20	50	—	80	540
Bradford	..	450	1,550	420	2,650	5,360
Castleford	..	100	50	—	50	840
Dewsbury	..	10	230	—	140	770
Halifax	..	440	380	50	400	1,940
Huddersfield	..	250	430	120	590	2,390
Keighley	..	40	100	220	180	850
Leeds	..	1,360	3,730	870	7,120	11,120
Morley	..	40	20	—	60	640
Shipley	..	10	60	20	50	880
Spenborough		50	200	—	70	550
Wakefield	..	240	200	40	310	1,300

Town		Public works contracting	Gas, water, and electricity supply	Railway service	Tramway and omnibus service	Road transport
Batley	..	30	180	50	10	80
Bradford	..	690	930	910	1,170	1,490
Castleford	..	440	150	70	90	180
Dewsbury	..	870	280	70	980	230
Halifax	..	330	700	80	780	510
Huddersfield	..	290	830	130	980	500
Keighley	..	40	250	50	20	120
Leeds ..	..	2,380	2,740	1,460	1,800	2,570
Morley	..	520	40	70	10	100
Shipley	..	190	160	40	10	60
Spenborough		20	10	20	10	130
Wakefield	..	410	120	260	1,130	370

Town	Distributive trades	Commerce, banking, insurance, etc.	National government services	Local government services	Professional services
Batley ..	780	10	30	420	50
Bradford ..	18,560	480	350	2,170	1,050
Castleford ..	1,350	30	80	350	50
Dewsbury ..	1,830	60	60	620	120
Halifax ..	3,720	200	80	1,220	290
Huddersfield ..	5,810	140	90	1,440	490
Keighley ..	1,460	60	40	430	150
Leeds	26,240	1,360	1,100	2,900	2,550
Morley ..	780	10	30	130	20
Shipley ..	1,020	20	10	370	30
Spenborough	1,100	10	20	560	60
Wakefield ..	3,070	40	180	3,640	190

Town	Entertainments and sports	Hotels, public house, restaurant, etc., service	Laundries, dry cleaning, etc.	Total, all industries*
Batley ..	50	50	110	12,810
Bradford ..	720	1,510	1,670	116,660
Castleford ..	130	120	20	21,620
Dewsbury ..	130	110	920	20,260
Halifax ..	180	330	190	39,960
Huddersfield ..	250	370	370	51,900
Keighley ..	70	140	130	17,630
Leeds	1,600	3,460	2,040	184,460
Morley ..	30	40	20	13,360
Shipley ..	40	40	60	13,330
Spenborough	30	10	50	16,800
Wakefield ..	140	180	120	30,210

* Including other industries in addition to those given in
the table.

INDEX

For Product Safety Concerns and Information please contact our EU
representative GPSR@taylorandfrancis.com Taylor & Francis Verlag GmbH,
Kaufingerstraße 24, 80331 München, Germany

Printed and bound by CPI Group (UK) Ltd, Croydon, CR0 4YY
08/05/2025
01864408-0001